HOW MUSLIM WOMAN PRAY

Step by Step Illustrated Instruction on How to Pray in Islam with Arabic and English Transliteration

Muhammad Nasrul Haq

Copyright © 2024 **Muhammad Nasrul Haq**
All rights reserved.

THIS BOOK OR ANY PORTION THERE OF MAY NOT BE REPRODUCED OR USED IN ANY MANNER WHATSOEVER WITHOUT THE EXPRESS WRITTEN PERMISSION OF THE PUBLISHER EXCEPT FOR THE USE OF BRIEF QUOTATIONS IN A BOOK REVIEW.

FIRST PRINTING, 2024

بِسْمِ اللَّهِ الرَّحْمَنِ الرَّحِيمِ

In the Name of Allah, the Most Gracious and the Most Merciful

اللَّهُمَّ صَلِّ عَلَى مُحَمَّدٍ، وَعَلَى آلِ مُحَمَّدٍ، كَمَا صَلَّيْتَ عَلَى إِبْرَاهِيمَ وَعَلَى آلِ إِبْرَاهِيمَ، إِنَّكَ حَمِيدٌ مَجِيدٌ

Allahumma Salli 'ala Muhammadin wa 'ala Ali Muhammmadin, kama sallaita 'ala Ibrahima wa 'ala aliIbrahima, Innaka Hamidum Majid.

"O Allah! Send Your Salawat (Graces, Honours and Mercy) on Muhammad and on the family of Muhammad, as You send Your Salawat on Ibrahim and on the family of Ibrahim, for You are The Most Praiseworthy, The Most Glorious."

Alhamdulillah, we are delighted to compile this book to be very knowledgeable to educate Muslims and non-Muslims on the topic of Prayer.

This book enables the readers to adapt the main aspects of prayer in Islam. It has been written in a very simple way so that people can attain the Islamic information on prayer very easily. It shows us how to obey, Allah (swt) in the manners which the Prophet Muhammad (saw) has taught us.

We have inserted practical illustration and stories related based on Sahih Hadith in prayers which will be outstanding and will be very beneficial to gain correct knowledge of Prayer.

This book will be perfect for Muslims and non-Muslims who have doubts about prayers in Islam. This book will also perfectly suit for young children to know about Why? When? Who? And how to Pray.

I make Du'a to Allah (swt) to keep the reader of this book and all Muslimin in the world safe and may He reward those sincere to Him in this world and hereafter, Ameen!!!

Table of Content

1. History of Salah………………………..…………….....Pg 4
2. When should my child start Salah…………………....……Pg 6
   - Guide on Teaching Kids to Salah
3. Who Should Perform Salah……………………………….Pg 9
4. Why we Perform Salah……………….....………..………Pg 10
   - Salah as a reminder
   - Salah and your heart
   - Salah erases sin
   - The Importance of Salah
   - Abandoning Salah
5. When we Perform Salah…………………………....………Pg 16
   - Adhan Calling of Salah
   - Meaning and how to answer Adhan
   - Iqamah
6. Purification Before Salah……………………………...…..Pg 27
   - Menstruation/Hayd for women
   - Salah Before & After Hayd
   - Purify Body & Cloth
   - How to Perform Wudhu / Ablution
   - Ghusl (Ritual bath) for Women
7. How to Perform Salah………………………………..…....Pg 42
   - Steps in offering Salah
   - What to do After Salam/Tasleem
8. Salah In Congregation…………………..………....Pg 63
   - What to do if Forgotten a Step
   - When to recite Aloud or Silently
   - What to do if Miss Salah
9. What do movements in Salah means……………....……Pg 66
10. Short 6 Surahs in Quran…………………………...……Pg 68
11. Congregational Prayer at home (standings)…………….…Pg 75
12. My Salah Tracker………………………………..……..Pg 81

HISTORY OF SALAH

Salah is one of the central elements of Islamic practice and worship. Indeed, it is the second of the Five Pillars of Islam.

This story was mentioned by Ibn Hishaam in As-Seerah, quoting Ibn Is-haaq. Ibn Is-haaq said:

"Some scholars related to me that when the prayer was enjoined on prophet Muhammad (saw) Jibril (as) (Gabriel) came to him in the upper part of Makkah. Jibril (as) hit the ground in the valley with his heel, so a spring of water gushed out, and Jibril (as) performed ablution while Prophet Muhammad (saw) was looking at him to learn the manner of ablution for the prayer. Then Prophet Muhammad (saw) performed ablution in the same manner as he saw Jibril (as) perform it. Then Jibril (as) stood and led him in prayer and then left. Afterwards, Prophet Muhammad (saw) came to Khadeejah (ra), and he performed ablution in order to show her how to perform ablution for the prayer as Jibril (as) had shown him. So she performed ablution in the like manner as prophet (saw) had done, and then Prophet Muhammad (saw) led her in the prayer in the same manner as Jibril led him in it."

Since that, prophet Muhammad (saw) began to pray two cycles (rakaah) of ritual prayer twice a day – once in the morning and once in the evening. From that time forward, the Prophet never went through a day without praying.

In the ninth year of the Prophet's mission, he was taken by the archangel Jibril on a miraculous journey by night to Jerusalem and from there, ascended to the heavens and the Divine Presence. During this tremendous journey, Allah (swt) commanded the Prophet (saw) and his followers to observe the ritual-prayer 50 times a day. Returning from the Divine Presence, Prophet Muhammad (saw) met Prophet Moses (as) who said,

"Seek a reduction, for your people can not carry it."

The Prophet did so and it was granted. After many such dialogues the command was reduced to observe 5 prayers, which would be the equivalent of the original command to observe fifty. For this reason, Muslims feel a great debt to Prophet Moses (as) for this intercession on their behalf.

In the morning after the night in which prayer was made obligatory. Jibril (as) came to Prophet (saw) when the sun had passed its zenith and said

"Get up, O Muhammad"

Then was when the sun had passed the meridian for Zuhr Then he waited until the (length of) a man's shadow was equal to his height, then he came to him for 'Asr and said

"Get up, O Muhammad and pray 'Asr"

Then he waited until the sun set, then he came to him and said

"Get up and pray Maghrib"

So he got up and prayed it when the sun had set fully. Then he waited until the twilight had disappeared, then he came and said

"Get up and pray 'Isha'"

so he got up and prayed it.

In this hadeeth it says: Jibril (as) said

"The period between two of these two times is the time to pray."

WHEN SHOULD MY CHILD START SALAH

As a responsible and cared parents, we should start teaching children to pray salah at the earliest but we are commanded to start at the age of 7. At that age children could understand and ready to learn. The obligatory salah are the first step to ensuring that we raise our children right.

Training, reminding and encouraging are the best before a child can form the habit to pray on time. It will not be an easy task to form this habit to pray 5 times a day daily. Even the adults still struggle to perform the salah on time.

We should start the journey and guide them step by step, gently, with as much love, together with modern teaching methods to make the learning curve fun and educational.

Prophet Muhammad (saw) taught with love and compassion. We should always teach our own children without any force, calm as possible and remember they are just children in learning stage.

We are commanded to start calling a child to pray from the age of 7 years and then from age 10 we should make them understand the real reason for praying, why we pray and the benefits of praying (salah).

Guide on Teaching Kids to Salah

We must always remember their age and level of understanding before we guide them to the habit of praying. Allah (swt) commanded us to start from the age of 7. We must always be the best example for them to follow and creating an environment for daily prayer will always help.

1. Show them from early on praying is a way of life. It is always difficult for parents to pray with a baby. Remind yourself at such time that children are a test from Allah (swt). Pray with the baby in your lap. Be persistent. Pray for ease. Make babies often watch with wonder when we stood up to pray. Let them hear the Adhan and see how prayer being performed. Habit of hearing and seeing prayer will develop anxiety.

2. From the age of 1 to 2 years. Let them sit next to you with toys while you pray. Toddlers need distractions because at prayer times they will feel like they aren't getting attention, so give them something that will keep them busy. You can get them their own little Musalla and head covering (scarf or cap) to wear. If you don't hear the Adhan as often, then make arrangements so the children know the timings of the Adhan easily.

3. From 3 to 5 years. Even if their speech is not much developed you can teach them small Du'as and zikr. Teach them the Adhan and the Iqamah (if they are little boys). They love to copy adults, let them pray with you. Teach them to do wudhu (supplication) when they are around 5 years old.

4. From age 6 show them how to perform their prayer correctly. No doubt prayer becomes obligatory only once the children are 7 years of age. That is the age when they are more willing to pray actually, so encourage it.

5. From 7 onwards, children will need to be often reminded to pray. The main reason can be they neglect their prayer is because they don't want to leave their play. Teach them more details and why we need to pray and to Allah we should seek help and guidance.

6. From 10 onwards, your child, if he is a boy, should be going to mosque. Girls can pray at home. Encouraging children to pray at this age can be a bit challenging because they are growing up and want to exercise their right on opinion. The best way to counteract this is to have clear rules in the household on what is expected of them and then help them in creating reminders so they don't forget. Pocket charts and visual wall charts are all good reminders.

Prophet Muhammad (saw) said:
(Abu Dawood & Ahmad)

"Teach your children to pray when they are seven years old, and smack them (lightly) if they do not pray when they are 10 years old, and separate them in their beds."

With regard to smacking a child for not praying, it is stipulated that the smacking should be light and should not be painful and should not break the skin, tooth or bone. It should be on the back or the hand, Face is to be avoided because it is forbidden to strike it, because the Prophet Muhammad (saw) forbid that. It should be done for the purpose of discipline and teaching.

WHO SHOULD PERFORM SALAH

Salah, is an obligation of the faith, it's a must performed 5 times a day by any adult Muslims.

Allah (swt) says:

"I created the jinn and humankind only that they might worship Me"

Surah Adh-Dhariyat (51:56)

Every adult Muslim who has reach puberty must perform the 5 daily fardh prayer. The signs of puberty are as follow

1. Wet dreams

2. Pubic hair

3. Menstruation (for girls)

4. Reaching the age of 15 (lunar years)

There are exceptional for women having their menstruation (monthly or after delivery) to pray. Anyhow the prayers that have been left must be completed once the menstruation ends.

Islam prohibits women to pray or fast during this period to reduce the burden and Islam understand the situation they are going through.

It is compulsory for a sick person to Salah according to his capabilities. If he is able to observe it like the healthy people, then he must do so, but if he is not capable, then observes it according to his strength.

WHY WE PERFORM SALAH

Salah is one of the fundamental pillars of Islam. It is the second priority for the Muslims after belief in the Shahadah (There is no god but Allah and Muhammad is the messenger of Allah). It is such an important pillar, that Muslims are called upon to perform this act of worship in all circumstances without fail.

Prophet Muhammad (saw) said:
(Jami At-Tirmidhi, Vol 5)

"Between a slave (of Allah) and disbelief is abandoning the Salah."

"The covenant between us and them is the Salah, so whoever abandons it he has committed disbelief."

When we talk about salah, what is actually salah means. The Arabic word Salah means 'To Pray', 'to supplicate or invoke.

'Salah' is the name given to the formal prayer of Islam, it means to worship Allah through certain known and prescribed sayings and actions, Starts with saying

'Allahu Akbar' (Allah is the Greatest)

and ends with saying

'As-Salaamu Alaykum Wa Rahmatullah' (May the peace, and mercy be upon you).

Salah as a reminder

Allah (swt) says:

"Verily, I am Allah! There is no God but Me, so worship Me, and perform As-Salah for My remembrance."

Surah Taha (20:14)

Salah reminds us About our Creator, Sustainer and Master – Allah, The Exalted and Glorified, the uniqueness of His names and attributes and His right of being the Only One worthy of worship.

Salah reminds us about The Creator Allah (swt) blessings upon us

Salah reminds us to seek forgiveness for our sins

Salah reminds us to correct ourselves and to follow Allah (swt) commandments

Salah reminds us to seek guidance and success in life and hereafter

Salah reminds us to be thankful to Allah (swt) for everything given in life.

Salah and Your Heart

Heart is a unique vital organ created by Allah inside every human body. The uniqueness of this is that, it is the only organ which is continuously at work from the time it is formed in the fetus inside the mother's womb, until the person's death.

If this beautiful machine (heart) stops its mechanism in order to take some rest, the person dies. Hence it needs rest without pausing its functioning. Allah (swt) has made Salah as the 'Rest to the Heart' of believers, for their hearts find comfort on the side of Allah, become peaceful when He is remembered and are pleased to have Him as their Protector and Supporter.

"Those who have believed and whose hearts are assured by the remembrance of Allah. Unquestionably, by the remembrance of Allah hearts are assured.

Surah Ar-Ra'd (13:28)

Salah Erases Sins

Prayer purifies the heart and truly, through Prayer, a believer attains spiritual devotion and moral elevation. Prayer not only gives a deep connection with Allah (swt), but in prayer one establishes patience, humility and sincerity. Prayer provides a means of repentance and is a restrainer from shameful and unjust deeds.

Prophet Muhammad (saw) said:
(Bukhari Muslim)

"If a person had a stream outside his door and he bathed in it five times a day, do you think he would have any filth left on him?"

The people said,

"No filth would remain on him whatsoever."

The Prophet (saw) then said,

"That is the example of the five Salah (daily compulsory prayers) with which Allah blots out (annuls) evil deeds (as long as major sins are avoided)."

The Importance of Prayer

Direct communication with Allah

Through prayer, you are able to connect with Allah(swt). Don't cut this relationship between you and your Creator.

Prophet Muhammad (saw) said:

"When any one of you stands to pray, he is communicating with his Lord, so let him pay attention to how he speaks to Him."

Success lies in the Prayer

Prophet Muhammad (saw) said:

"The first of his deeds for which a man will be called to account on the Day of Resurrection will be the prayers. If it is found to be perfect, he will be safe and successful. But if it is defective, he will be unfortunate and a loser."

Makes us humble

Realising Allah (swt) greatness and dependence on our Lord, man is humbled and rids us from pride and arrogance.

Cures our Problems

Man is surrounded by numerous trials and problems. Once we focus on strengthening our relationship with Allah (swt), Who is All-Powerful, will fix our worldly problems.

Abandoning Prayer

Disobeying your Creator

This is the most serious and obvious consequence. The whole purpose of your existence is to worship Allah, yet you are disobeying your Creator every day.

Being ungrateful

Refusing the invitation of your Creator to establish this close relationship is the ultimate ingratitude. Allah (swt) created you and gave you everything.

Being lazy

The Creator of the heavens and the earth, The One who blessed you with 24 hours and still breathing, yet only need to spend about 30 minutes a day for prayer.

Only harming yourself

Allah (swt) doesn't need your prayer. Allah doesn't need anything from anyone Glory be to Him. It is we that stands in need of His mercy.

Allah (swt) said

"Be grateful to Allah, and whoever be grateful, it is only for his own soul's good, and whoever is ungrateful, surely Allah is Free of all needs, Worthy of all praise."

Surah Luqman (31:12)

WHEN WE PERFORM SALAH

Allah (swt) has Gifted upon His slaves 5 prayers throughout the day and night at specific times. This gift had been awarded to the Ummah of Prophet Muhammad (saw). It is time given for remembrance and to seek success. They are for the heart of human as like water for a tree, given to it time after time, not all in one go and then it stops. The prayers have been split within day and night so that people will not to get bored or find it too difficult, which would happen if they all had to be done at once.

Prophet Muhammad (saw) said:
(Muslim)

"The time for Zuhr is from when the sun has passed its zenith and a man's shadow is equal in length to his height, until the time for 'Asr comes. The time for 'Asr lasts until the sun turns yellow. The time for Maghrib lasts until the twilight has faded. The time for 'Isha' lasts until midnight. The time for Subh (Fajr) prayer lasts from the beginning of the pre-dawn so long as the sun has not yet started to rise. When the sun starts to rise then stop praying, for it rises between the two horns of the Shaytaan."

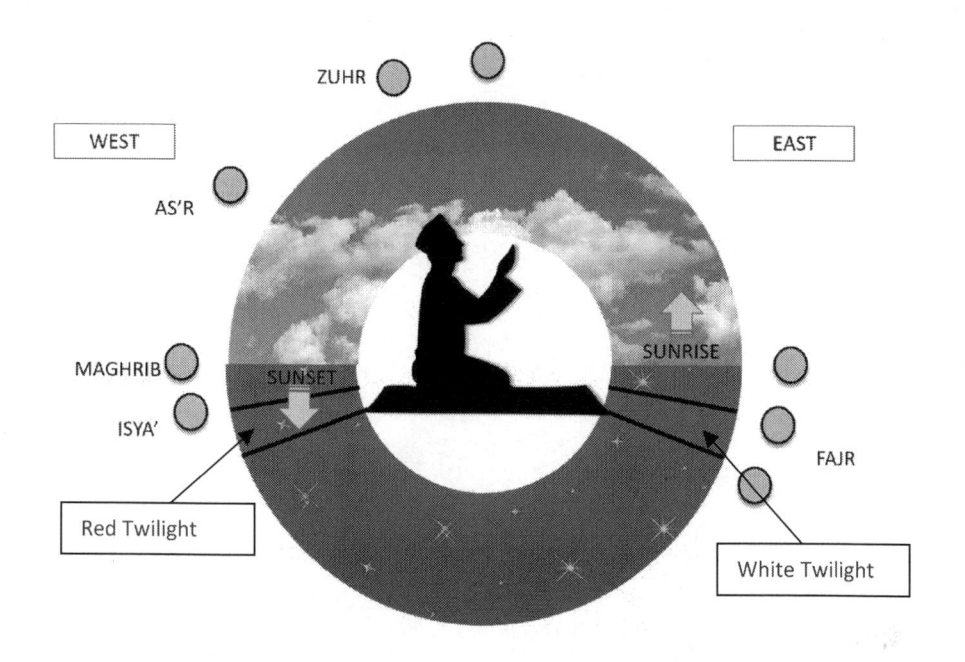

Compulsory Prayer 5 Times a day (Fardh)

Fajr – After dawn Until before Sunrise
(When white twilight of Fajr appear)

Zuhr – After Sun declines from Zenith till As'r
(When the sun moves from the meridian and the shadow is extended)

As'r – Midway between Noon till Sunset
(When the shadow is equal to shadows length)

Maghrib – Immediately after sunset before dusk
(When the sun moves below the horizon)

Isya' – After Dusk until before dawn
(When the red twilight disappears)

Adhan Calling of Salah

Muslim communities are reminded of the salah by the daily calls for fardh prayer, known as adhan. Adhan" in Arabic means conveying. The adhan are delivered from mosques by a muazzin, the mosque's designated caller of prayer. During the call to prayer, the muazzin recites the Takbir and the Kalimah.

It is not permitted for a **woman** to give the call to prayer (adhan), even if among only women, however, it is sunnah for a woman to call the commencement of prayer (iqama), and this is recommended whether she is praying alone or in a women congregation.

When Prophet Muhammad (saw) and the Muslims of Makkah had made hijrah to Madinah and the First Mosque built by prophet (saw) Masjid Al- Nabi, the Muslims used to come and wait for the time of salah to be announced by the Prophet (saw) so that they could all go and pray.

In Makkah, the number of Muslims was small, so they could make Jama'ah without any call, but by the second year of Hijrah, the number of Muslims had increased. At first the people announced in a loud voice, "As-Salat ul-Jami'ah" (The salah for jama'ah is ready). Those who heard this call came to join the Salah.

Muslims felt the need to find a way to inform people to come to prayer. It was quite difficult for the Muslims to know when to stop what they were doing and pray. Some lived far away from the masjid al-Nabi, and found it even harder, because they would have to travel far to be able to find out when it was going to be prayer time.

One day, Prophet Muhammad (saw) asked the Muslims about a way to call everyone for prayer (salah) five times a day.

some suggested.

"We could use a horn, like the Jews do,"

Suggested by others

"What about using a bell to call Muslims, the Christians use a bell,"

There have been many various ideas given such as putting a big fire, raise a flag and so on, but the Prophet (saw) didn't like those ideas and disagreed with it.

Eventually, Prophet Muhammad (saw) decided that out of all the suggestions, the bell was the best one, and thought to buy a bell. However, Prophet Muhammad (saw) was still not satisfied about the problem, and unhappy that they were unable to find a good solution for calling people to salah.

The next morning, a bell had not yet been brought to call the Muslims. Perhaps they were still trying to think of an answer to their problem.

While the blessed Prophet (saw) was sitting in the masjid with his Companions, a companion by the name of Abdullah ibn Zaid (r.a) walked in.

"Assalamu 'alaykum," he said, greeting the Prophet (saw) and all his companions happily.

"Wa alaikum assalam warahmatullah," replied the Prophet (saw), and his companions.

"You look so happy this morning Abdullah ibn Zaid," "let us share your happiness." said one of companion to him,

Replied Abdullah ibn Zaid

"Last night I saw a dream, A beautiful dream. In all my life, I have never seen a more beautiful dream than that."

The Companions were intrigued and very curious as to what Abdullah ibn Zaid could have dreamt of. They asked

"Tell us about your beautiful dream Abdullah!"

Abdullah ibn Zaid said:

"I saw in my dream, a man dressed with green clothes, carrying a bell,

I asked: Will you sell me your bell?'

The man said: Why you needed a bell

I said: I needed a bell to call people for salah

He said: You don't need a bell. Let me teach you something better than a bell

I said: Please do, May Allah bless you!

He said: You say loudly

Allahu Akbar, Allahu Akbar

Allahu Akbar, Allahu Akbar

اَللهُ اَكْبَر اَللهُ اَكْبَر

اَللهُ اَكْبَر اَللهُ اَكْبَر

Ashhadu alla ilaha illallah

Ashhadu alla ilaha illallah

اَشْهَدُ اَنْ لَّا اِلٰهَ اِلَّا الله

اَشْهَدُ اَنْ لَّا اِلٰهَ اِلَّا الله

Ash-hadu anna Muhammadar Rasul-Allah

Ash-hadu anna Muhammadar Rasul-Allah

اَشْهَدُ اَنَّ مُحَمَّدًا رَّسُولُ الله

اَشْهَدُ اَنَّ مُحَمَّدًا رَّسُولُ الله

Hayya 'alas salaah,

Hayya 'alas salaah,

حَيَّ عَلَى الصَّلٰوة

حَيَّ عَلَى الصَّلٰوة

Hayya 'alal falaah,

Hayya 'alal falaah,

حَيَّ عَلَى الْفَلَاحْ

حَيَّ عَلَى الْفَلَاحْ

Allahu Akbar, Allahu Akbar

اَللهُ اَكْبَر اَللهُ اَكْبَر

La illaha il-Allah

لَا اِلٰهَ اِلَّا الله

The Prophet (saw) and the Muslims were very happy with Abdullah ibn Zaid's dream. It was indeed a beautiful dream.

Then the Prophet (saw) called Bilal ibn Rabah (ra), a freed Abyssinian slave, because he had a loud and beautiful voice, and taught him the beautiful and meaningful words of the Adhan. When Bilal ibn Rabah (ra) had learnt the words, Prophet Muhammad (saw) asked him to climb a high wall next to the masjid, and call people for Salah, and Bilal did what the Prophet (saw) told him to do.

The voice of Bilal (ra) resounded throughout Madinah. People came running to Masjid un-Nabi. Umar (ra) was one of the persons who came and said,

"O Messenger of Allah, an angel taught me the same words in my dream last night."

From that day forward, Bilal (ra) became the first Muazinn of Islam, all the Muslims around the world call the Adhan five times a day, just like Bilal did.

Additional phares adhan for fajr prayer will be

As-salaatu Khairum Minan Naum (The prayer is better than sleep)

As-Salaatu Khairum Minan Naum (The prayer is better than sleep)

Meaning and how to answer Adhan

اَللّٰهُ اَكْبَرُ اَللّٰهُ اَكْبَرُ

Allahu Akbar Allahu Akbar (Recited 2 times)
"Allah is the Greatest, Allah is the Greatest"

*Answers the call of "Allahu Akbar, Allahu Akbar"
by repeating it by saying "Allahu Akbar Allahu Akbar"*

اَشْهَدُ اَنْ لَّا اِلٰهَ اِلَّا اللّٰه

Ashhadu alla ilaha illallah (Recited 2 times)
"I bear witness that there is none worthy of worship except Allah"

*Answers the call of "Ashhadu alla ilaha illallah"
by repeating it by saying" "Ashhadu alla ilaha illallah"*

اَشْهَدُ اَنَّ مُحَمَّدًا رَّسُولُ اللّٰه

Ashhadu anna Muhammadar Rasulullah (Recited 2 times)
"I bear witness that Muhammad is the Messenger of Allah."

*Answer the call of "Ashhadu anna Muhammadar Rasulullah"
by repeating it by saying "Ashhadu anna Muhammadar Rasulullah"*

حَيَّ عَلَى الصَّلٰوةِ

Hayya 'alas-Salah (recited 2 times)
"Come to Prayer"

*Answer the call of "Hayya 'alas-Salaah"
by saying "La haula wala quwwata illa billa-hil 'aliyyul azim"
Means "There is neither might nor any power except with Allah"*

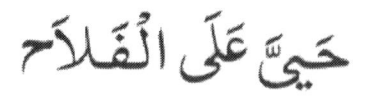

حَيَّ عَلَى الْفَلَاحِ

Hayya 'alal-falah (recited 2 times)
"Come to success"

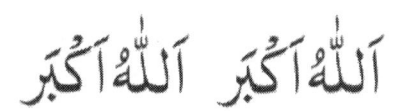

*Answer the call of "Hayya 'alal-faalah"
by saying "La haula wala quwwata illa billa-hil 'aliyyul azim"
Means "There is neither might nor any power except with Allah"*

اَللّٰهُ اَكْبَرُ اَللّٰهُ اَكْبَرُ

Allahu Akbar Allahu Akbar

*Answers the call of "Allahu Akbar, Allahu Akbar"
by repeating it by saying "Allahu Akbar Allahu Akbar"*

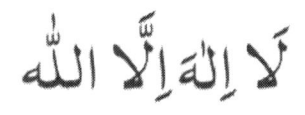

لَا اِلٰهَ اِلَّا اللّٰهُ

La ilaha illallah

"There is none worthy of worship except Allah."

Iqamah

اَللهُ اَكْبَرُ اللهُ اَكْبَرُ، اَشْهَدُ اَنْ لَّا إِلٰهَ إِلَّا الله، اَشْهَدُ اَنَّ مُحَمَّدًا رَّسُولُ اللهِ، حَيَّ عَلَي الصَّلٰوةِ، حَيَّ عَلَى الْفَلَاحِ، قَدْ قَامَتِ الصَّلٰوةُ قَدْ قَامَتِ الصَّلٰوةُ، اَللهُ أَكْبَرُ اللهُ أَكْبَرُ، لَا إِلٰهَ إِلَّا اللهُ۔

Allahu Akbar, Allahu Akbar, Ashhadu alla Ilaha illallah, Ashhadu anna Muhammadar Rasulullah, Hayya 'alas-Salah, Hayya 'alal-Falah, Qad qamatis-Salatu, Qad qamatis-salah, Allahu Akbar Allahu Akbar, La Ilaha Illallah

"Allah is the Greatest, Allah is Greatest; I bear witness that there is none worthy of worship except Allah; I bear witness that Muhammad is the Messenger of Allah. Come to Prayer. Come to success. Salat is ready. Allah is the Greatest; Allah is the Greatest; There is none worthy of worship except Allah."

After completion of the Adhaan/iqamah, listeners should recite the following prayer

اللَّهُمَّ رَبَّ هَذِهِ الدَّعْوَةِ التَّامَّةِ وَالصَّلَاةِ الْقَائِمَةِ آتِ سَيِّدَنَا مُحَمَّدٍ الْوَسِيلَةَ وَالْفَضِيلَةَ وَالشَّرَفَ وَالدَّرَجَةَ الْعَالِيَةَ الرَّفِيعَةَ وَابْعَثْهُ مَقَامًا مَحْمُودًا الَّذِى وَعَدْتَهُ إِنَّكَ لَا تُخْلِفُ الْمِيعَادِ.

"Allahumma Rabba hazhihidda'watit-tammati,wassalatil qa'imati,ati sayidina Muhammada-nil-wasilata wal-fadhilata washarafa wadha rajatal a'liyatal rafi'ah wab'ath-hu maqamam-mahmuda al-ladhi wa'adtha inakala tukhliful miadh"

"O Allah! Lord of this perfect call and of the regular Salah (prayer) which is going to be established! Kindly give Muhammad Al-Wasilah (highest position in Paradise) and Al-Fadilah (extra degree of honour) and raise him to Maqam Mahmud You have promised (a station of praise and glory) You never break Your promise"

Abdullah bin Amr bin Al-As reported:

Prophet Muhammad (saw) said:
(Sahih Muslim)

"When you hear the Adhaan, repeat what the Muazzin says. Then ask Allah(swt) to exalt my mention because everyone who does so will receive in return ten rewards from Allah(swt). Then beseech Allah(swt) to grant me Al-Wasilah, which is a high rank in Jannah, fitting for only one of Allah's slaves; and I hope that I will be that man. If anyone asks Al-Wasilah for me, it becomes incumbent upon me to intercede for him."

PURIFICATION BEFORE SALAH

Allah (swt) said

"A mosque founded on righteousness from the first day is more worthy for you to stand in. Within it are men who love to purify themselves; and Allah loves those who purify themselves."

Surah At- Taubah (9:108)

To perform your Salah you must be clean and pure, some of the Impurities that must be removed before performing Salah, Such as

- Human Disposal/bladder.
- Wadi (A thick white secretion that might be discharged after Urination)
- Mathi (A white sticky prostatic fluid, other than sperm or semen).
- Menstrual blood.
- Defecation and urine of animals

Before performing salah, make sure cleaned from minor hadath and major hadath, purification is very important before we stand to meet The Almighty ALLAH (swt)

MENSTRUATION/HAYD FOR WOMEN

Menstruation is a natural process which takes place in woman's body every month. Allah has created the woman such that she plays the major role in the perpetuation of the human race.

The primary reproductive organs of a woman are her ovaries. When a girl is born, her ovaries already contain about 400,000 immature eggs (which are known as ova). At puberty, the eggs start maturing, usually one ovum each month. The maturing of the ovum takes place roughly halfway between two menstrual cycles. After maturing, it finds its way from the ovary to the fallopian tube and ends up in the womb. It is a very normal biological process that ensures the perpetuation of the human race and it got nothing to do with curse or sins.

Some women will feel uncomfortable a few days before and during menstruation. This discomfort is caused by some of the biological changes which take place in the woman's body.

Allah (swt) said

"It is harm, so keep away from wives during menstruation. And do not approach them until they are pure. And when they have purified themselves, then come to them from where Allah has ordained for you. Indeed, Allah loves those who are constantly repentant and loves those who purify themselves"

Surah Al- Baqarah (2:222)

Definition of Hayd

There are four possible causes for discharge of blood from women:

1. Menstruation. (Hayd)
2. Loss of virginity.
3. Post-natal bleeding.
4. Internal injury.

In the Islamic terminology, menstruation is known as hayd. And a woman who is having her period is known as hayd. and according to Islamic laws, menstruation is the process of discarding the endometrium which normally takes place once a month in women from the day they attain puberty until they reach the age of menopause.

The Signs: If a woman is not sure about the nature of her discharge, then she should look for the follow-ing three signs of the menstrual blood:

- Warmth
- Dark red or black colour
- Pressure and slight burning in the discharge.

If these three signs are found together, then it is menstruation.

Duration of Hayd

The beginning of menstruation is determined when blood leaves the uterus and enters the vagina. It is necessary for the commencement of menstruation that the blood should be seen outside the vagina. The minimum duration of menstruation is three days, and the maximum is ten days

Although it is normal to say that menstruation takes place once "a month", but it should be clarified that menstrual cycles take place every 28 days - so, in the present context "a month" means a period of 28 days, not 29, 30 or 31 days.

Forbidden during Hayd

Menstruation is the flow of blood; and blood, is an unclean substance and so menstruation is also considered unclean. But the impurity of menstruation in no way prevents a woman from living a normal life with her family and friends.

There are certain acts of worship in Islam which are so sacred that a Muslim, whether man or woman, cannot perform them unless he or she has certain qualifications.

A woman who is in her periods is excused from salah (prayers) because she does not have an important qualification for salah, (cleanliness). She does not even have to perform them later on as qada'. Likewise, a hayd woman is excused from fasting; but in this case, she has to fast after the month of Ramadhan as qada.

Allah (swt) said

"Allah does not intend to make difficulty for you, but He intends to purify you and complete His favor upon you that you may be grateful."

Surah Al- Maidah (5:6)

Salah Before & After Hayd

Whenever a woman sees blood, she should stop her salah - of course, if she discovers later on that it was not hayd, then she should perform qada of the salah which she had missed.

If the time for a particular salah has already begun and a woman fears that by delaying the salah her period may start, then it is wajib on her to perform that salah immediately.

If the time for a particular salah has already begun and the woman did not pray until her period started, then she has to perform that salat as qada after the menstruation stops and she becomes clean.

If a woman's period starts while she is engaged in salah, her prayer will be invalid.

If a woman who is engaged in salah doubts whether or not her period has started, her doubt will have no effect on the salah unless she discovers later on that her period had actually begun.

If a woman becomes pure from menstruation and has enough time to perform ghusl and pray, at least, one rak'ah in time then it is wajib on her to do so. In case she does not pray, then it will be wajib on her to perform its qada.

Purify Body and Cloth

Generally, water will be used to purify anything that is impure. One must remove all impurities from his/her private parts by using any pure matter. Priority must be water or both.

This is performed by washing them with water until they are cleansed of impurities (cleaned from visibility, smell and colour). This is especially important in the case where the impurity is visible, such as menstrual blood. If there are some difficult stains that remain after washing, they can be overlooked. If the impurity is not visible, such as urine, it is sufficient to wash it once, but preferable to wash it three times.

Purifying clothing infected by male infant's urine can be performed by sprinkling water on the stained clothing. If itis stained by the urine of a female infant, then it must be washed. Infant who breastfeeds and below 2 years old only.

Bottom of shoes must be purified by rubbing them against the ground until the remains impurity are removed.

Utensils/ Human body must be purified if they were touched by dog saliva or forbidden meat (pork). This must be performed by using soil and water 7 times.

Cleanliness are essentials for the body, clothing, and place of worship. It has to be free of Hadath (ritual impurities).

There are two kinds of Hadath (Ritual Impurities)

1. Minor Hadath:

Minor impurity nullifies Wudu (Ablution). It happens after one or more of the following occurs: natural discharges like urine, excrement, passing gas, falling asleep, or unconsciousness of any kind.

2. Major Hadath:

Major impurity nullifies washing the whole body (ghusl). It could be caused by unconscious ejaculation (e.g. in one's sleep), intercourse, menstruation or post-childbirth bleeding. This type of washing requires bathing the whole body, including, the head with pure water.

Allah (swt) said

"O you who have believed, when you rise to [perform] prayer, wash your faces and your forearms to the elbows and wipe over your heads and wash your feet to the ankles. And if you are in a state of janabah, then purify yourselves. But if you are ill or on a journey or one of you comes from the place of relieving himself or you have contacted women and do not find water, then seek clean earth and wipe over your faces and hands with it." Allah does not intend to make difficulty for you, but He intends to purify you and complete His favour upon you that you may be grateful.

Surah Al Maidah (5:6)

How to Perform Wudhu (Ablution)

Before we perform Salah we must first prepare ourselves. This preparation includes making sure that we are clean from any physical impurities and performing Wudhu. Wudhu (ablution) is required for performing Salah. We cannot offer our Salah without first making Wudu.

Here are the steps to take:

1. First, make the Niyyah (intention) in your heart that this act of Wudu is for the purpose of preparing for Salah, and say: "Bismillah" (in the name of Allah).

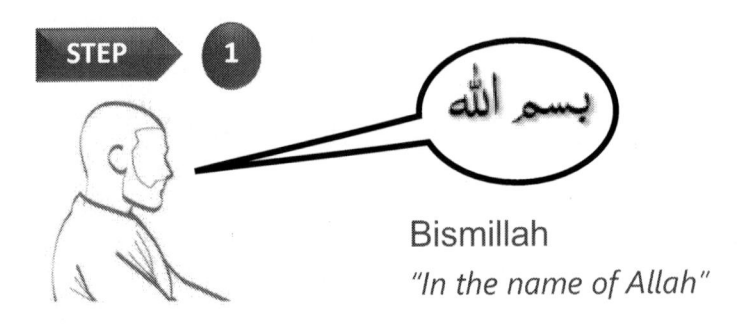

STEP 1

بسم الله

Bismillah
"In the name of Allah"

2. Wash both hands up to the wrists (starting with the right hand) 3 times, making sure that water has reached between the fingers.

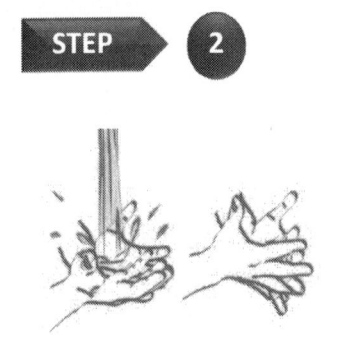

STEP 2

3. Take water with your right hand, put it into your mouth and rinse thoroughly 3 times.

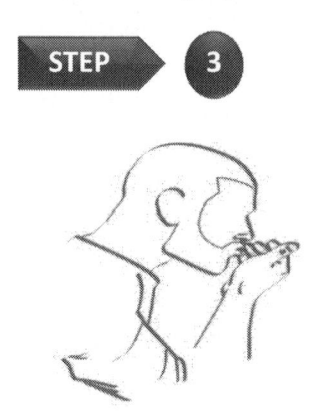

STEP 3

4. Take water with your right hand, splash it into your nose and blow it out 3 times. (Use the left hand if necessary to help blow it out).

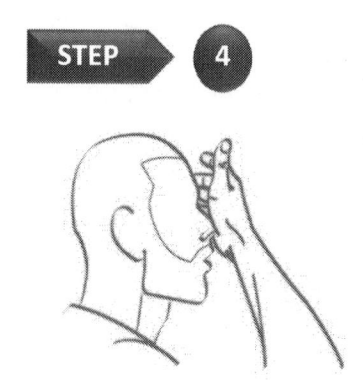

STEP 4

5. Take water wash your whole face 3 times repeatedly. (The whole face from the end right ear to the end left ear, and edge of the forehead to the bottom of the chin).

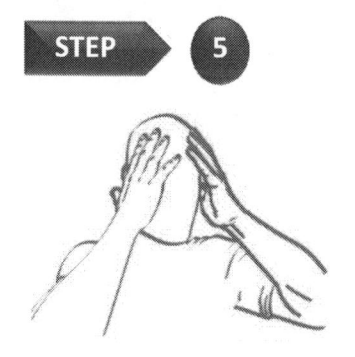

STEP 5

6. Wash the right arm thoroughly from end of finger to elbow 3 times, and make sure that no part of the arm has been left unwashed. Repeat the same with the left arm. (always start with right arm then left arm)

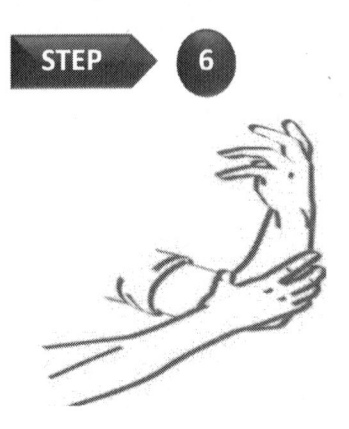

STEP 6

7. Move the palms of the wet hands lightly over the head, starting from the top of the forehead to the back of the head, and passing both hands over the back of the head to the neck, and then bringing them back to the forehead. (3 times)

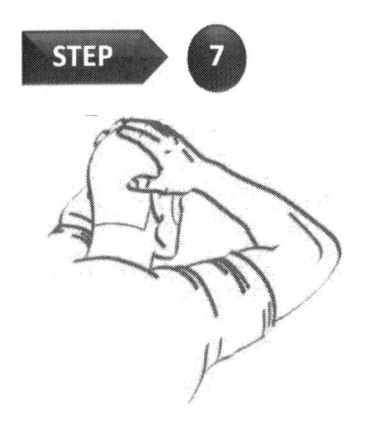

STEP 7

8. Then rub the grooves and holes of both ears with the wet index fingers, while also passing the wet thumbs behind the ears from the bottom upward. (3 times)

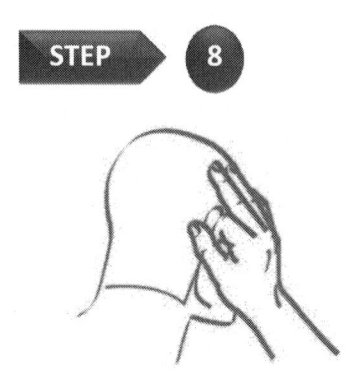

STEP 8

9. Finally, wash both feet to the ankles 3 times, starting with the right foot then left foot. Make sure that water has reached between the toes and covered the rest of the foot

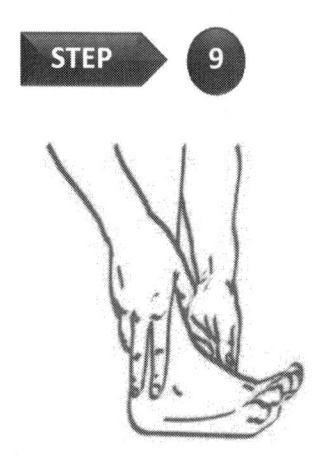

STEP 9

If you put on your socks, shoes, or sandals (only those that cover most of the foot) while you have a valid Wudu, it is not necessary to take them off every time you need to renew your Wudu. You can leave them on and wipe the top of each covered foot once with wet hands in place of washing the entire foot.

STEP 10

اشْهَدُ انْ لَّا إِلَهَ إِلَّا اللهُ وَ اَشْهَدُ اَنَّ مُحَمَّدًا اعَبْدُه وَرَسُولُهُ

Ash'hadu an la ilaha illallahu wahdahu la sharika lahu, wa ash'hadu anna Muhammadan 'abduhu wa Rasuluh.

"I bear witness that none has the right to worshipped but Allah, with no partner or associate, and I bear witness that Muhammad is his slave and Messenger"

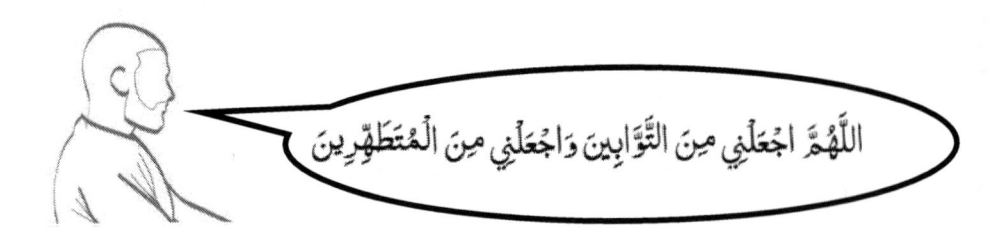

اللَّهُمَّ اجْعَلْنِي مِنَ التَّوَّابِينَ وَاجْعَلْنِي مِنَ الْمُتَطَهِّرِينَ

Allahummaj 'alni minat-tawwabina waj'alni minal mutatahhirin

"Oh Allah, make me among those who turn to You in repentance, and make me among those who are purified"

Wasting water while performing Wudu is prohibited. As Allah (swt) does not like those who extravagant.

Ghusl (Ritual Bath) For Women

Ghusl means washing the entire body with water and it is obligatory on a person in the following cases:

1. If there is discharge of semen due to stimulation or because of an erotic dream (wet dream).
2. Females are required to perform ghusl when their menstruation period end.
3. Females are required to perform ghusl at the end of their post childbirth bleeding. If she continues to sleep for more than 39 days, then she must perform ghusl at the end of the 40th day.
4. It is required to perform ghusl on a Muslim who has died but if the Muslim died as a Shaheed then no ghusl is required.

Niyyah (Intention) of Ghusl

It is SUNNAH to make the niyyah for Ghusl

One should make the intention of becoming clean from that impurity he wishes to get himself clean from.

Requirement in Ghusl

Passing water into and out of the mouth, i.e. gargling

Putting water into the nostrils

Passing water over the whole entire body.

* If a Fardh is left out, or a hair's-breadth place is left dry, the Ghusl will be incomplete.

5 sunnah in Ghusl

1. Washing hands up to the wrists
2. Washing the private parts and the parts over which uncleanliness is found
3. Niyyah (intention) of washing off any unseen filth
4. Making wudhu before washing the body
5. Then passing water over the whole body thrice.

Rules in Performing Ghusl

- Ghusl should be made in a place of total privacy.
- One should not face Qiblah while making Ghusl.
- Ghusl may be performed standing or seated, preferably seated.
- Use sufficient water - do not skimp nor be wasteful.
- Abstain from speaking whilst making Ghusl.
- It is better not to read any Kalimah or Ayah while bathing.
- Before performing Ghusl, one should make niyyah.

* Without niyyah, there is no Sawaab (reward) although Ghusl will be valid.

Procedure in Ghusl

1. Wash both hands, including the wrists.
2. Wash the private parts, If there is visible filth elsewhere on the body, it should now be washed off.
3. Perform Wudhu (Ablution as of before Salah)
4. Pour water over the head three times
5. Pour water over the right shoulder three times and left shoulder three times.
6. Then pour water over the entire body and rub.

It is compulsory to wet all the entire body end to end. If a single hair is left dry, **Ghusl will not be valid.**

It is Mustahab (preferable) to clean the body by rubbing it. All parts of the body should be rubbed with the hands to ensure that water has reached all parts of the body and no portion is left dry.

Rings, earrings, etc., should be removed to ensure that no portion covered by them is left dry. Ensure that the navel and ears are all wet. If they are not wet, Ghusl will be incomplete.

On completion, one should confine oneself to a clean place. If, while performing Wudhu, the feet had been washed, it is not necessary to wash them again. Dry the body with a clean towel and dress as hastily as possible.

If after Ghusl one recalls that a certain portion of the body is left dry, it is not necessary to repeat the entire Ghusl. Merely wash the dry portion. It is not sufficient to pass a wet hand over the dry place. If one has forgotten to rinse the mouth or the nostrils, these too must be rinsed when recalled after Ghusl has been performed.

HOW TO PERFORM SALAH

The Compulsory and Sunnah Prayers

Prayer	Before(Sunnah)	Compulsory	After(Sunnah)
Fajr	2	2*	
Zuhr	2	4	2
As'r	2	4	2
Maghrib		3*	2
Isya'	2	4*	2

Rak'ah or units for each of the 5 daily prayers

Note: The Quranic recitation of the first two rak'ah or units in the prayers which have black asterisk (*) mark, should be recited aloud. All other rak'ah or units of these prayers should be recited silently (without disturbing other Jama'ah).

The salah for Zuhr on Friday are called Friday prayer, it will be performed 2 rak'ah instead of 4. It must be performed in a Jamaah (group of people). The Juma'ah prayer will be started with a Khutbah by the Khatib/imam which is a must for all the muslim to attend. It is a session where we gain more knowledge about Islam and a reminder for all of us.

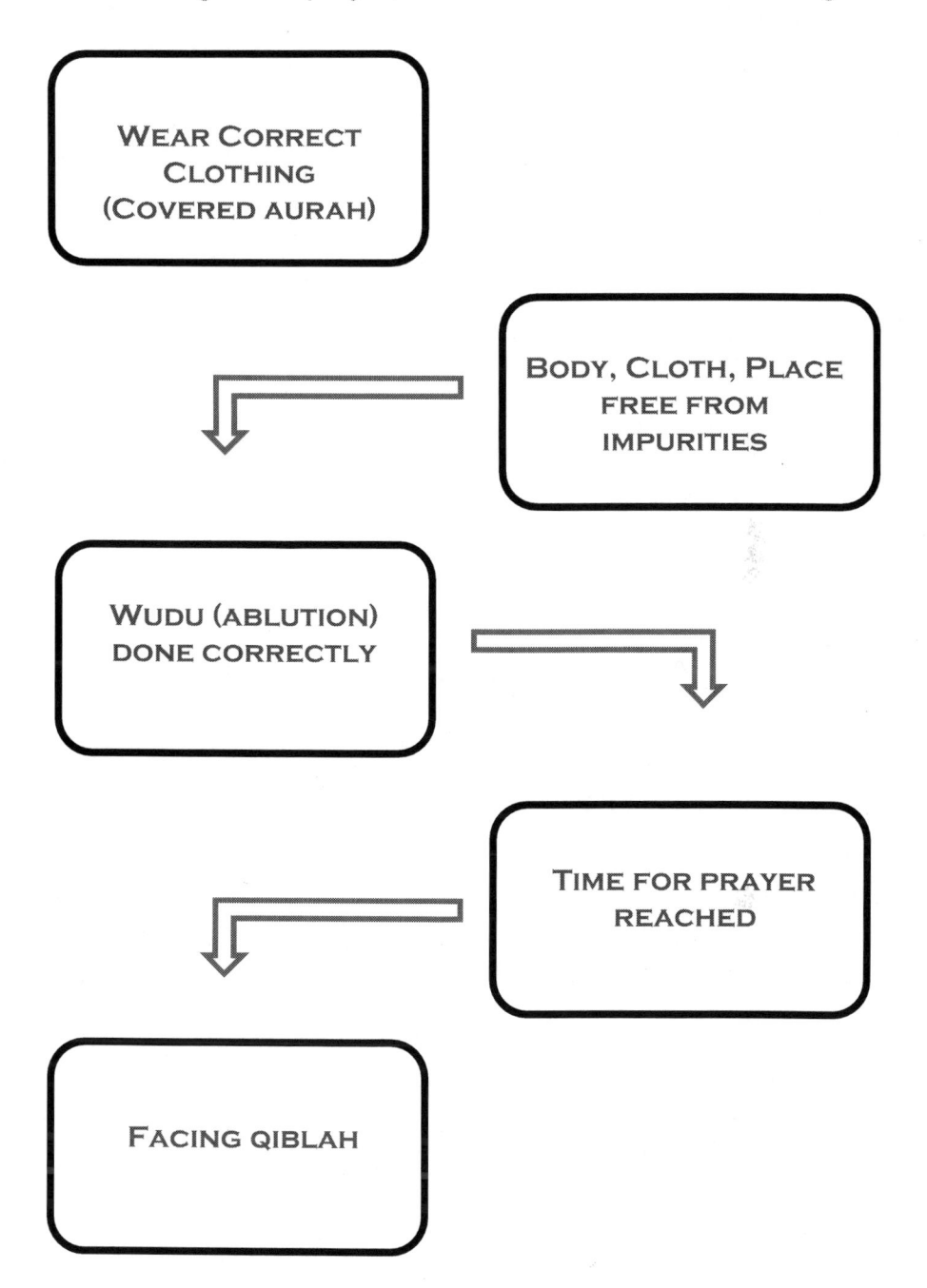

Before we begin with prayer, we must make sure the following

- **Wear Correct Clothing (Covered aurah)**
- **Body, Cloth, Place free from impurities**
- **Wudu (ablution) done correctly**
- **Time for prayer reached**
- **Facing qiblah**

Before you begin your Salah, however, you must make sure that you have a clean body, a clean place to pray, and that you are wearing clothing free of impurities.

The minimum clothing required during Salah is:

A man must cover the front and back of his body between his navel and knees, It is preferable to cover his shoulders when praying. The garment must be clean, loose and non-transparent.

A woman must cover her entire body, except for her hands(wrists) and face. The garment must be

Clean

Loose (Does not shows the shape of any parts of body)

Non-transparent.

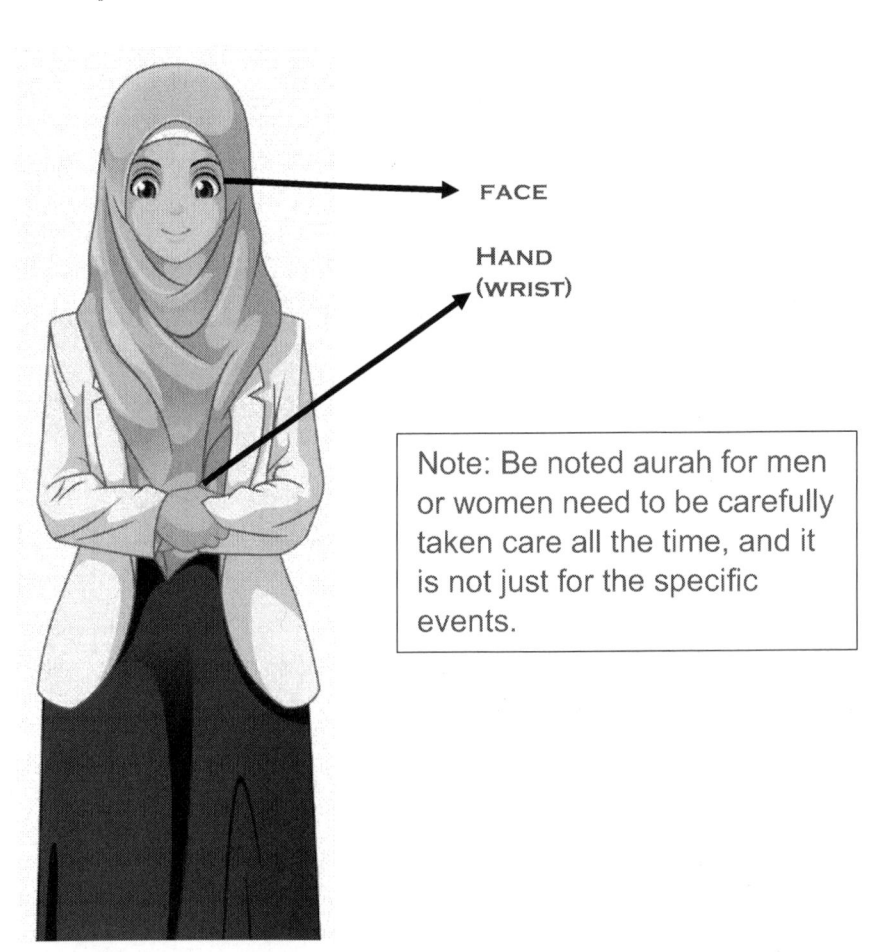

FACE

HAND (WRIST)

Note: Be noted aurah for men or women need to be carefully taken care all the time, and it is not just for the specific events.

Steps in offering Salah

Stand upright straight facing the direction of Ka'bah. Make Niyyah (intention) about the particular obligatory or optional prayer intend to be perform. Raise both hands (palms facing the Qiblah) Up to your earlobes or shoulder and say: "Allahu Akbar". This is called Takbiratul Ihram.

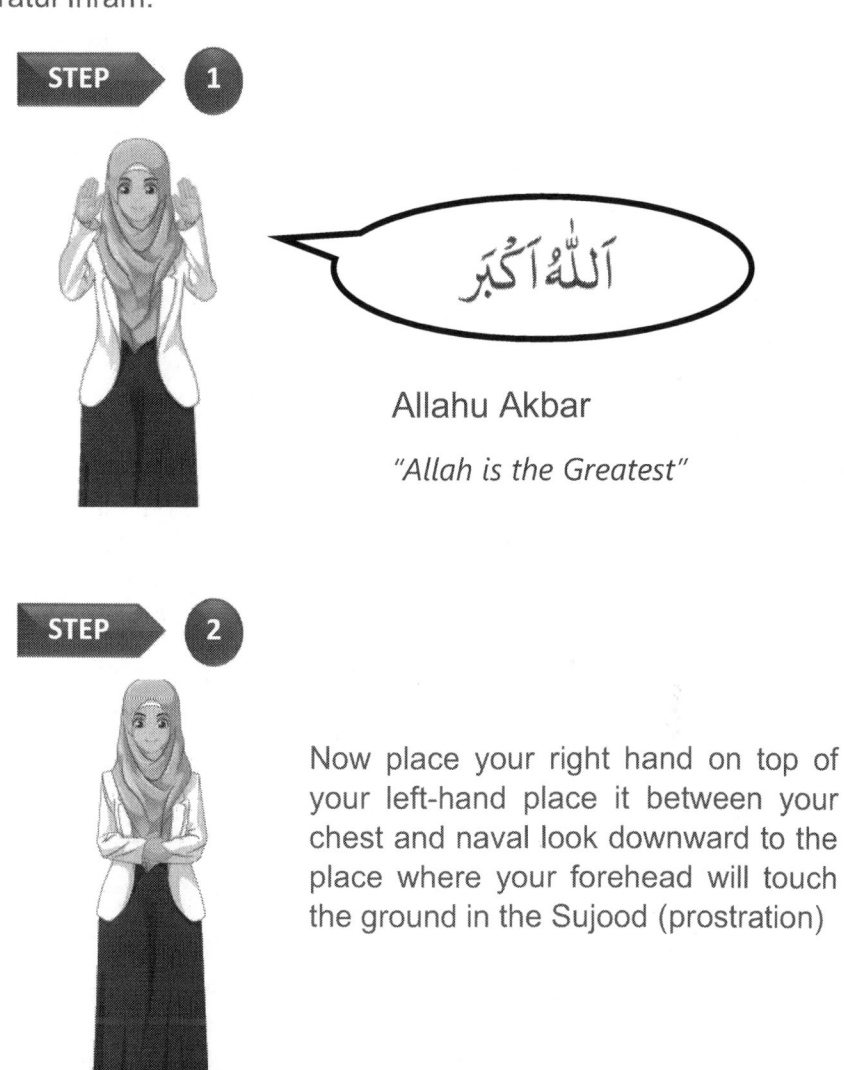

STEP 1

اَللّٰهُ اَكْبَر

Allahu Akbar

"Allah is the Greatest"

STEP 2

Now place your right hand on top of your left-hand place it between your chest and naval look downward to the place where your forehead will touch the ground in the Sujood (prostration)

STEP 3 — Recite Iftitah

اللهُ أَكْبَرُ كَبِيرًا، وَالْحَمْدُ لِلَّهِ كَثِيرًا،
وَسُبْحَانَ اللهِ بُكْرَةً وَأَصِيلاً،
وَجَّهْتُ وَجْهِيَ لِلَّذِى فَطَرَ السَّمَوَاتِ وَالأَرْضَ
حَنِيفًا وَمَا أَنَا مِنَ الْمُشْرِكِينَ،
إِنَّ صَلَاتِي وَنُسُكِي وَمَحْيَايَ وَمَمَاتِي لِلَّهِ رَبِّ الْعَالَمِينَ
لَا شَرِيكَ لَهُ وَبِذَلِكَ أُمِرْتُ وَأَنَا مِنَ الْمُسْلِمِينَ.

Allahu Akbar kabira Walhamdu lillahi katheera, Wa subhana allahi bukratan wa asila, wajjahtu wajhiya lilladhi fataras-samawati wal ardh hanifan wama ana minal mushrikin, Inna solati wanusuki wamahyaya wamamati lillahi rabbil alamiin, la sharika lahu wabi zalika umirtu wa ana minal muslimin,

"Allah is Greater and praise be to Allah and glory be to Allah, in the evening and the morning, have turned my full attention towards the Supreme Being, Who has created the heavens and the earth, and I am not one of those who associate partners with Him. For sure my prayer, my submission, my life and my death because of Lord of Universe. There is no partner with Him and this is what I have been commanded (to profess and believe) and I am of the believers"

STEP 4 — Continue Recite Surah Al-Fatiha

بِسْمِ ٱللَّهِ ٱلرَّحْمَٰنِ ٱلرَّحِيمِ

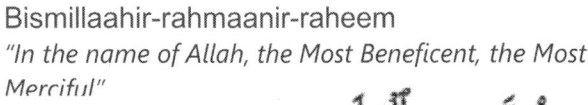

Bismillaahir-rahmaanir-raheem
"In the name of Allah, the Most Beneficent, the Most Merciful"

ٱلْحَمْدُ لِلَّهِ رَبِّ ٱلْعَٰلَمِينَ

Alhamdulillaahi rabbil 'aalameen
"Praise be to Allah the Lord of the Worlds"

ٱلرَّحْمَٰنِ ٱلرَّحِيمِ

Ar-rahmaanir-raheem
"The Most Beneficent, the Most Merciful"

مَٰلِكِ يَوْمِ ٱلدِّينِ

Maaliki yawmiddeen
"Master of the Day of Judgement"

إِيَّاكَ نَعْبُدُ وَإِيَّاكَ نَسْتَعِينُ

Iyyaaka na'budu wa iyyaaka nasta'een
"You alone we worship and in You alone we seek help"

ٱهْدِنَا ٱلصِّرَٰطَ ٱلْمُسْتَقِيمَ

Ihdinas-siraatal mustaqeeme
"Guide us to the straight path"

صِرَٰطَ ٱلَّذِينَ أَنْعَمْتَ عَلَيْهِمْ غَيْرِ ٱلْمَغْضُوبِ عَلَيْهِمْ وَلَا ٱلضَّآلِّينَ

Siratallatheena an'amta 'alayhim Ghayril maghdoobi 'alayhim Walathaalleen
"The way of those whom You have favored Not the way of those who have earned Your anger Nor of those who have gone astray"

Aameen *"O Allah, answer our prayers!"* آمِين

STEP 5

Now Recite another chapter from the Qur'an. Reciting Surah only on the 1st and 2nd Rak'ah (Unit). In the 3rd and 4th Rak'ah (Unit), only recitation of the Fatihah is required

*Some short chapters from the Qur'an have been given at the end of this chapter.

STEP 6   Now going into Rukoo

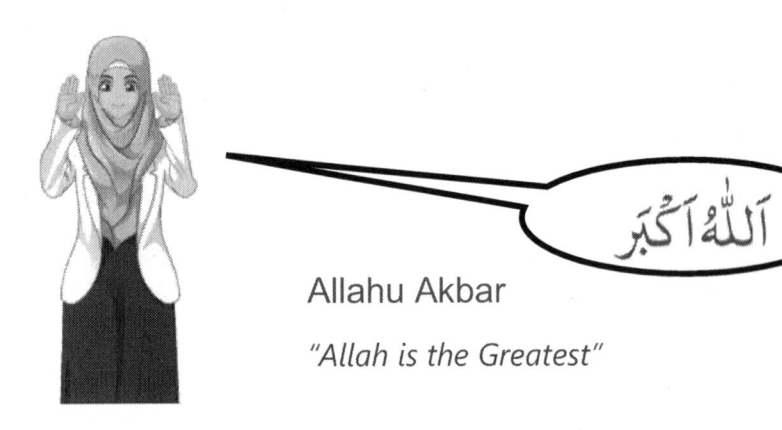

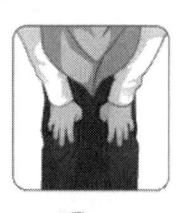

اَللّٰهُ اَكْبَر

Allahu Akbar

"Allah is the Greatest"

Now bow down and place your hands on your knees and say 3 times

سُبْحَانَ رَبِّيَ الْعَظِيم

Subhaana rabbiyal 'atheem

"Glory be to my Lord the Supreme"

STEP 7 Now rise up from the bowing position into standing position.

While rising up recite.

سَمِعَ اللهُ لِمَنْ حَمِدَهُ

Sami'-Allaahuliman hamidah

"Allah listens to the one who praises"

Now you should be in the standing position with your hands by your sides. Once you are standing straight recite

رَبَّنَا وَلَكَ الْحَمْدُ

Rabbanaa wa lakal hamd

"Our Lord, and to You belongs the praise"

STEP 8

Next, go into the prostration (sujood) position, as you going to sujood say

Allahu Akbar
"Allah is the Greatest"

اَللّٰهُ اَكْبَرْ

In the sujood position say 3 times

سُبْحَانَ رَبِّيَ الْأَعْلَى

Subhaana rabbiyal a'laa *"How Perfect is my Lord, the Highest"*

In the prostration position (sujood), make sure the followings
- The nose and forehead are touching the ground
- The two palms are on the floor with fingers together
- The two knees are on the floor
- Both feet are kept together.
- The toes of both feet are in the direction of the qiblah

Prophet Muhammad (saw) said:

"Do the prostrations properly and do not put your forearms flat with elbows touching the ground like a dog"

[Sahih Bukhari]

STEP 9

Next, come up into sitting position, while coming up say

اَللّٰهُ اَكْبَرُ

Allahu Akbar
"Allah is the Greatest"

اللَّهُمَّ اغْفِرْ لِي، وَارْحَمْنِي،
وَاهْدِنِي، وَاجْبُرْنِي، وَعَافِنِي،
وَارْزُقْنِي، وَارْفَعْنِي

Allaahum-maghfirli, warhamnee, wahdinee, wajburnee, wa a'finee, warzuqnee, warfa'nee.

"O Allah! Forgive me, have mercy on me, guide me, support me, protect me, provide for me and elevate me."

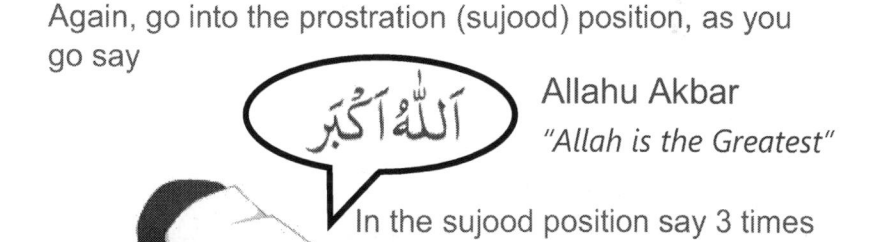

STEP 10

Again, go into the prostration (sujood) position, as you go say

اَللّٰهُ اَكْبَرُ

Allahu Akbar
"Allah is the Greatest"

In the sujood position say 3 times

سُبْحَانَ رَبِّيَ الْأَعْلَى

Subhaana rabbiyal a'laa
"How Perfect is my Lord, the Highest"

STEP 11

This completes the first Rak'ah or unit of Salah. Now stand up for the second Rak'ah and while standing up say

$$\text{اَللهُ اَكْبَر}$$

Allahu Akbar
"Allah is the Greatest"

Place your right hand on top of your left hand on the chest as the same action done on step 1&2

Continue to Step 4 and perform it the same way except in the 2nd rak'ah (unit) don't have to recite supplication du'a. Straight recite surah Al-Fatiha

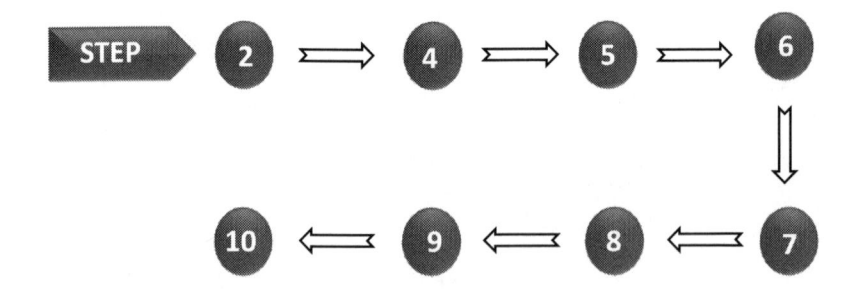

STEP 2 ⇒ 4 ⇒ 5 ⇒ 6
10 ⇐ 9 ⇐ 8 ⇐ 7

STEP 12

After completing again, the step 2 to 10 in 2nd rak'ah, instead standing up, you must be in sitting position as in step 9. While raising from prostration (sujood) say

اَللهُ اَكْبَرُ

Allahu Akbar

"Allah is the Greatest"

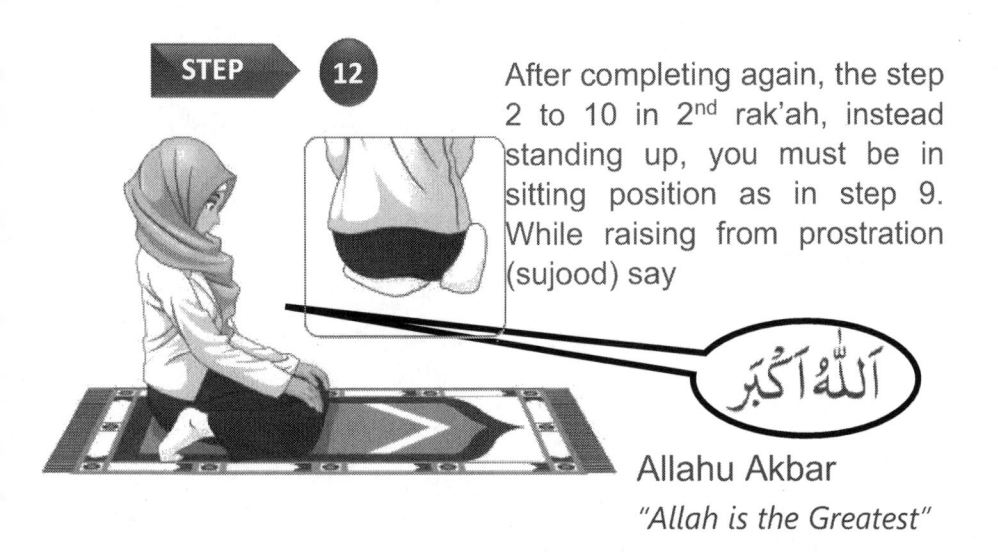

This position is known as first Tashahhud. Recite as follows

التَّحِيَّاتُ الْمُبَارَكَاتُ الصَّلَوَاتُ الطَّيِّبَاتُ لِلهِ، السَّلَامُ عَلَيْكَ أَيُّهَا النَّبِيُّ وَرَحْمَةُ اللهِ وَبَرَكَاتُهُ، السَّلَامُ عَلَيْنَا وَعَلَى عِبَادِ اللهِ الصَّالِحِينَ، أَشْهَدُ أَنْ لَا إِلَهَ إِلَّا اللهُ وَأَشْهَدُ أَنَّ مُحَمَّدًا رَسُولُ لِلهِ، اللَّهُمَّ صَلِّ عَلَى مُحَمَّدٍ.

Attahiyya tulmubaraka tuthsalawa tuthoiyiba tulillah, Assalamulalaika ayyuhan nabi yu warahmatullah hi wabarakatuh, Assalamualaina wa'ala ibadillahi solihin, Ash-hadu allaa ilaaha illallaah, Wa ash-hadu anna Muhammadan 'rasulullah, Allahumma solli a'ala Muhammad.

"All compliments, prayers and pure words are due to Allah, Peace be upon you Oh Prophet and the mercy of Allah and His blessings, Peace be upon us and on the righteous slaves of Allah, I bear witness that there is no God or deity worthy of worship except Allah and I bear witness that Muhammad is Messenger of Allah"

The rak'ah (unit) for each fard prayer will determine the next step in completing the prayers. For Fajr prayers there are only 2 raka'ah so rather than continuing the step 12, we should straight go to step 13 completing last Tashahud.

STEP 13

After completing first tashahhud, rise back to the standing position for continuing the 3rd and 4th. While saying

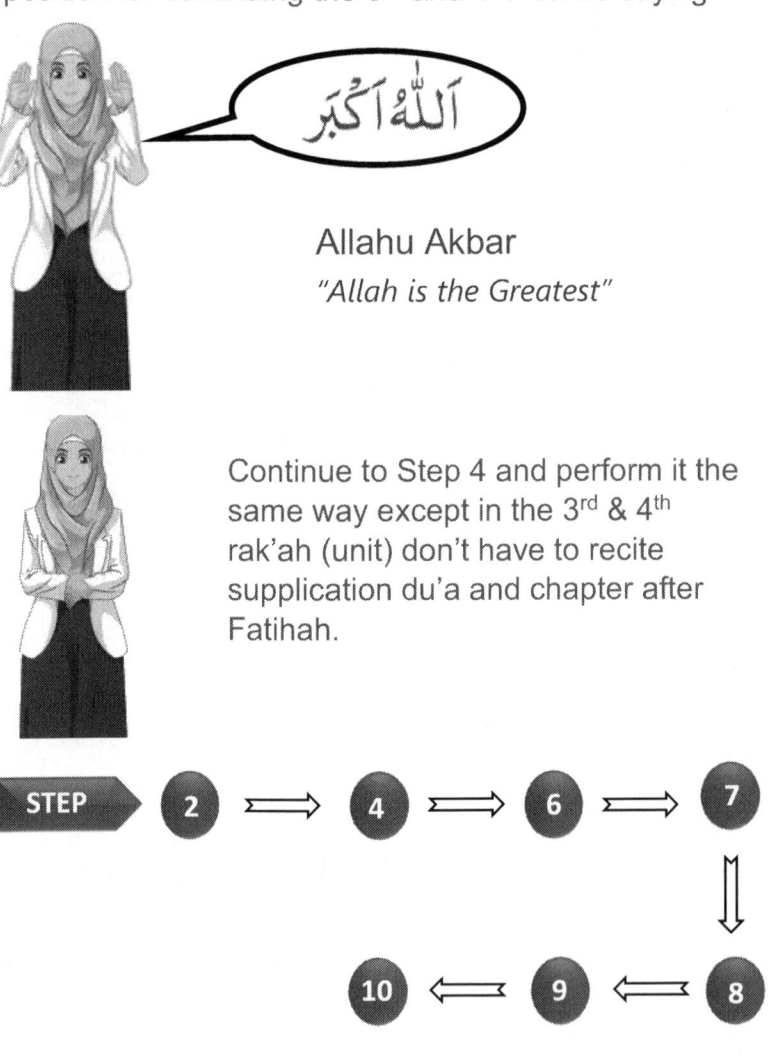

اَللّٰهُ اَكْبَر

Allahu Akbar
"Allah is the Greatest"

Continue to Step 4 and perform it the same way except in the 3rd & 4th rak'ah (unit) don't have to recite supplication du'a and chapter after Fatihah.

STEP 2 ⇒ 4 ⇒ 6 ⇒ 7
⇓
10 ⇐ 9 ⇐ 8

STEP 14 Completing the Last Tashahhud. While coming from sujood to this position for the last Tashahud say,

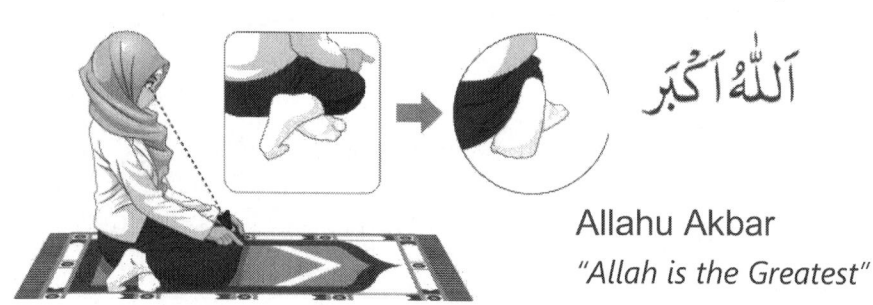

اَللّٰهُ اَكْبَرُ

Allahu Akbar

"Allah is the Greatest"

This position is known as Last Tashahhud. Recite as follows

التَّحِيَّاتُ الْمُبَارَكَاتُ الصَّلَوَاتُ الطَّيِّبَاتُ لِلّٰهِ، السَّلَامُ عَلَيْكَ أَيُّهَا النَّبِيُّ وَرَحْمَةُ اللهِ وَبَرَكَاتُهُ، السَّلَامُ عَلَيْنَا وَعَلَى عِبَادِ اللهِ الصَّالِحِينَ، أَشْهَدُ أَنْ لاَ إِلَهَ إِلاَّ اللهُ وَأَشْهَدُ أَنَّ مُحَمَّدًا رَسُولُ اللهِ، اللَّهُمَّ صَلِّ عَلَى مُحَمَّدٍ وَعَلَى آلِ مُحَمَّدٍ كَمَا صَلَّيْتَ عَلَى إِبْرَاهِيمَ وَعَلَى آلِ إِبْرَاهِيمَ، وَبَارِكْ عَلَى مُحَمَّدٍ وَعَلَى آلِ مُحَمَّدٍ كَمَا بَارَكْتَ عَلَى إِبْرَاهِيمَ وَعَلَى آلِ إِبْرَاهِيمَ فِي الْعَالَمِينَ، إِنَّكَ حَمِيدٌ مَجِيدٌ.

Attahiyya tulmubaraka tuthsalawa tuthoiyiba tulillah, Assalamulalaika ayyuhan nabi yu warahmatullah hi wabarakatuh, Assalamualaina wa'ala ibadillahi solihin, Ashhadu Allah ilaaha illallaah, Wa ash-hadu anna Muhammadar 'rasulullah, Allahumma solli a'ala Muhammad wa'ala ali Muhammad kama sollaita'ala Ibrahim wa'ala alilbrahim. Wabarik 'ala Muhammad wa'ala aliMuhammad. Kama barakta 'ala Ibrahim wa'ala ali Ibrahim. Fil 'alamin innaka hamidummajid.

"All compliments, prayers and pure words are due to Allah, Peace be upon you Oh Prophet and the mercy of Allah and His blessings, Peace be upon us and on the righteous slaves of Allah, I bear witness that there is no God or deity worthy of worship except Allah and I bear witness that Muhammad is Messenger of Allah"

O Allah, let Your mercy come upon Muhammad and the family of Muhammad as You let it come upon Ibrahim and the family of Ibrahim O Allah, bless Muhammad and the family of Muhammad as You blessed Ibrahim and the family of Ibrahim. Truly You are Praiseworthy and Glorious."

STEP 15 Completing the salah (Salam/tasleem)

Turn your head to the right and say

السَّلامُ عَلَيْكُمْ وَرَحْمَةُ الله

Assalaamu 'alaykum wa rahmatullah
"May Allah's peace and mercy be upon you"

Then, turn your head to the left and say

السَّلامُ عَلَيْكُمْ وَرَحْمَةُ الله

Assalaamu 'alaykum wa rahmatullah
"May Allah's peace and mercy be upon you"

What to do after Salam / Tasleem

After the salam, the Salah is completed. It is recommended to make supplication after the completion of prayer and Sunnah prayer whenever can and recite the zikr.

Great reward in making du'a (supplication) after the obligatory prayers. Prophet Muhammad (saw) was asked

"Which du'a is more heard (by Allah)?"

Prophet Muhammad (saw) said:
(At-tirmidzi)

"The du'a during the last part of the night and after the obligatory prayers." (At-Tirmidhi)

Sunnah for a Muslim to say after every obligatory prayer, whether he prayed as an imam or behind an imam (congregation) or alone

Recite 3 times

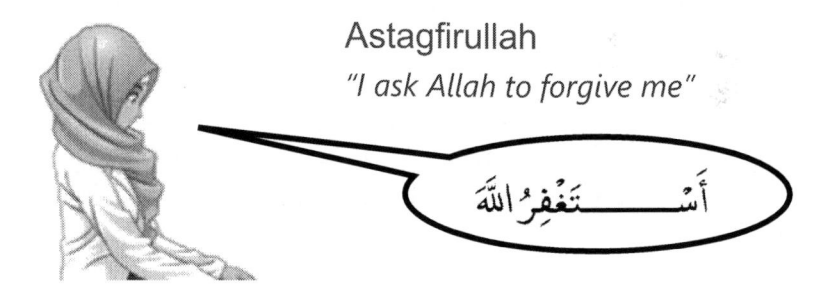

Astagfirullah
"I ask Allah to forgive me"

أَسْتَغْفِرُ اللَّه

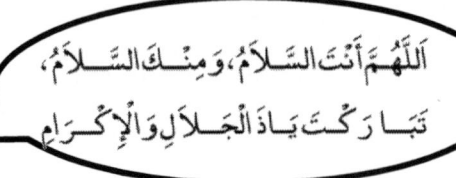

> اَللَّهُمَّ أَنْتَ السَّلَامُ، وَمِنْكَ السَّلَامُ، تَبَارَكْتَ يَاذَا الْجَلَالِ وَالْإِكْرَامِ

Alla'humma antas salaam wa min kas salaam taba rakta ya dhal ja laa li wal ik raam

"O' Allah, You are the Peace, and You are the Source of Peace, You are Blessed, Oh Possessor of Glory and Honor"

> اَللَّهُمَّ أَعِنِّيْ عَلَى ذِكْرِكَ، وَشُكْرِكَ، وَحُسْنِ عِبَادَتِكَ

Allahumma a'inni ala dhikrika wa shukrika wa husni ibadatika

"O' Allah Assist me in remembering you, in thanking you, and worshipping you in the best of manners"

لَا إِلَهَ إِلَّا اللَّهُ وَحْدَهُ لَا شَرِيكَ لَهُ، لَهُ الْمُلْكُ وَلَهُ الْحَمْدُ، وَهُوَ عَلَى كُلِّ شَيْءٍ قَدِيرٌ، لَا حَوْلَ وَلَا قُوَّةَ إِلَّا بِاللَّهِ، لَا إِلَهَ إِلَّا اللَّهُ، وَلَا نَعْبُدُ إِلَّا إِيَّاهُ، لَهُ النِّعْمَةُ وَلَهُ الْفَضْلُ، وَلَهُ الثَّنَاءُ الْحَسَنُ، لَا إِلَهَ إِلَّا اللَّهُ مُخْلِصِيْنَ لَهُ الدِّيْنَ وَلَوْ كَرِهَ الْكَافِرُونَ

La ilaha illa allahu wah dahu la shareeka laahu, lahul mulku wa lahul hamdu, wa huwa 'ala kullee shay'in qadeer, La hawla wa laqu-aata illah billah, la ilaha illAllah wala na'budu illayyah, lahun-ni'matu, wa lahul fadl, wa lahu-saana ul hasanu, la ilaha illAllahhu mukhliseena lahudeen, wa law karihal kafiroon.

"None has the right to be worshipped except Allah, alone, without partner, to Him belongs all sovereignty and praise and He is over all things omnipotent. There is no might nor power except with Allah, none has the right to be worshipped except Allah and we worship none except Him. For Him is all favour, grace, and glorious praise. None has the right to be worshipped except Allah and we are sincere in faith and devotion to Him although the disbelievers detest it."

Subhaan Allah 33 x سُبْحَانَ الله
"Glory be to Allah"

Al-hamdu lillah 33 x اَلْحَمْدُ لله
"Praise be to Allah"

Allahu Akbar 33 x اَللهُ أَكْبَرَ
"Allah is the greatest"

لاَ إِلَهَ إِلاَّ اللَّهُ وَحْدَهُ لاَ شَرِيكَ لَهُ، لَهُ الْمُلْكُ وَلَهُ الْحَمْدُ، وَهُوَ عَلَى كُلِّ شَيْءٍ قَدِيرٌ

La ilaha illallahu wahdahu la sharikalah, lahul-mulku wa lahul-hamdu wa huwa 'ala kulli shai'in qadir

"There is none worthy of worship but Allah alone, with no partner or associate; His is the Dominion, to Him be praise, and He is Able to do all things."

بِسْمِ اللّٰهِ الرَّحْمٰنِ الرَّحِيمِ

اللّٰهُ لَآ إِلٰهَ إِلَّا هُوَ الْحَىُّ الْقَيُّومُ ۚ لَا تَأْخُذُهُۥ سِنَةٌ وَلَا نَوْمٌ ۚ لَّهُۥ مَا فِى السَّمٰوٰتِ وَمَا فِى الْأَرْضِ ۗ مَن ذَا الَّذِى يَشْفَعُ عِندَهُۥٓ إِلَّا بِإِذْنِهِۦ ۚ يَعْلَمُ مَا بَيْنَ أَيْدِيهِمْ وَمَا خَلْفَهُمْ ۖ وَلَا يُحِيطُونَ بِشَىْءٍ مِّنْ عِلْمِهِۦٓ إِلَّا بِمَا شَآءَ ۚ وَسِعَ كُرْسِيُّهُ السَّمٰوٰتِ وَالْأَرْضَ ۖ وَلَا يَـُٔودُهُۥ حِفْظُهُمَا ۚ وَهُوَ الْعَلِىُّ الْعَظِيمُ

Bismillaahir Rahmaanir Raheem

Allahu laaa ilaaha illaa huwal haiyul qai-yoom; laa taakhuzuhoo sinatunw wa laa nawm; lahoo maa fissamaawaati wa maa fil ardh, man zallazee yashfa'u indahooo illaa be iznih, ya'lamu maa baina aideehim wa maa khalfahum, wa laa yuheetoona beshai 'immin 'ilmihee illa be maa shaaaa, wasi'a kursiyyuhus samaa waati wal arda wa la ya'ooduho hifzuhumaa, wa huwal aliyyul 'azeem

"Allah – there is no deity except Him, the Ever-Living, the Sustainer of [all] existence. Neither drowsiness overtakes Him nor sleep. To Him belongs whatever is in the heavens and whatever is on the earth. Who is it that can intercede with Him except by His permission? He knows what is [presently] before them and what will be after them, and they encompass not a thing of His knowledge except for what He wills. His Kursi extends over the heavens and the earth, and their preservation tires Him not. And He is the Most High, The Most Great."

اَللّٰهُمَّ صَلِّ عَلَى مُحَمَّدٍ وَعَلَى آلِ مُحَمَّدٍ، كَمَا صَلَّيْتَ عَلَى إِبْرَاهِيمَ وَعَلَى آلِ إِبْرَاهِيمَ، إِنَّكَ حَمِيدٌ مَجِيدٌ

Allah humma salli 'ala muhammadin wa'ala ali muhammadin, kama sal'layta 'ala ibraheema wa'ala ali ibraheema innaka hameedum majeed.

"O Allah, let Your Blessings come upon Muhammad and the family of Muhammad, as you have blessed Ibrahim and his family. Truly, You are Praiseworthy and Glorious."

SALAH IN CONGREGATION

Prayer in congregation is not obligatory for women, and a woman's prayer in her house on her own is better than her praying in congregation in the mosque. If congregational prayer is held in the house, then it is better for the woman to pray with them and not to pray alone, whether the congregation is women or men who are her mahrams.

Congregation of two people: The least amount of people needed to form a 'congregational' prayer is two people. If there are only two people praying, then the follower stands slightly behind the Imam, such that their toes are slightly behind the heel of the Imam. This applies to a male leading another man or a women leading another woman.

Congregation of three or more people: If there are three or more people in the female congregation, then the women stand in rows like men, and the female imam stands in the middle of the front row

Salah in a congregation will be rewarded more than salah alone. All gaps should be filled by connecting shoulders to shoulders and feet to feet.

Men should pray in front with or without other men. Women should pray behind the men, with or without other women. If a man and a woman are praying together, the woman should stand directly behind the man, not to his right. Imam's actions and statements should lead and should followed by others, and make sure never to get ahead of the imam in any action or step.

Arriving late to a congregation prayer and matched the Imam before he has risen from the position of Rukoo, then the Rak'ah is counted and follow the rest. However, if caught the Imam after he has risen from Rukoo, then must follow the Imam until salam but do not make salam, instead, get up and make-up the Rak'ah(s) that missed.

If in doubt about how many Rak'ahs' prayed, then just take the lower number as remembered, make up the remaining rak'ah and complete the salah with Sujood (prostration) Assahu in the end of the salah.

What to do if Forgotten Step

Sujood Assahu (The prostration of forgetfulness)
There are two extra Sujoods (prostration) that needs to be made at the end of prayer when you have forgotten an essential act/step.

These 2 Sujoods are just like the ones done in any prayer. Performing these Sujoods will make up for your mistake
By making two extra Sujoods just before Salam/Tasleem.

You make these extra Sujoods if you have done one or more of the following:
- If you forgot to do any essential Step/act
- If you added an extra step
- If you doubted on the Step you prayed

When to recite Aloud or Silently

During obligatory Fajr prayers, you recite Al-Fatihah and Qur'an surah aloud in both Rak'ahs. For Zuhr and Asr recite Al-Fatihah and Qur'an surah silently in all rak'ah. Prayer of Maghrib and Isya' recite aloud for first 2 rak'ah and recite silently on the following rak'ah. Furthermore, the one who leads Jumu'ah prayers (Friday prayer in place of Zuhr) will recite the Qur'an aloud.

It is sunna for a woman to recite aloud in prayers in which audible recitation is recommended, and this applies to when she is praying alone or in a female group. However, if non-mahram men are present, then she should recite to herself.

What to do if miss Salah

If you miss a prayer you have to make it up as soon as you wake up or remember. Prayers are compulsory and must be made up back(qada).

Prophet Muhammad (saw) said:
(Sahih Bukhari)

"The reward of the Salah (prayer) offered by a person in congregation is multiplied twenty-five times as much than that of the Salah offered in one's house or in the market (alone). And this is because if he performs ablution and does it perfectly and then proceeds to the mosque with the sole intention of offering Salah, then, for every step he takes towards the mosque, he is upgraded one degree in reward and his one sin is taken off (erased) from his accounts (of deeds). When he offers his Salht, the angels keep on asking Allah's Blessings and Allah's Forgiveness for him as long as he is (staying) at his Musalla (prayer place). They say, 'O Allah! Bestow Your Blessings upon him, be Merciful and kind to him.' And one is regarded in Salah as long as one is waiting for the Salah"

WHAT DO MOVEMENT IN SALAH MEANS

Niyyah (intention of prayer)

Niyyah is the decision of the heart, the declaration of the reasons behind each action. It means to intend saying 'yes' to Allah (SWT) by obeying His commands.

Takbir (The opening Takbir)

By saying Allahu Akbar ('Allah is Greater'), we toss the entire world behind us with our hands and seek refuge in the mercy of Allah (SWT). It is to affirm that Allah (SWT) is the greatest by saying takbir (Allahu Akbar). Clearly it's a submission or surrender to Allah (swt)

Qiyam (standing)

By standing straight, human beings represent the worship of the angels and of trees which stand and praise Allah continuously. Qiyam is the human beings' standing before the Eternal Being Allah (swt) with their bodies and hearts. The head's being bowed in qıyam represents the lack of pride and modesty of the heart.

Qira'at (recitation)

Qira'at is to be grateful to Allah (swt) for His flawless perfection, inimitable beauty and infinite mercy, by saying Alhamdulillah ('Praise be to Allah'). It is also to indicate that all deeds come into existence with the help of Allah and that praise is reserved for Allah (swt) alone.

Rukoo' (bowing)

In this state, human beings represent the worship of the angels who serve Allah in this position of bowing continuously, and animals that are always standing in rukoo on their four legs. Rukoo means to glorify the great Creator with the entire universe while seeing our weakness and poverty by saying, "Subhana rabbiyal 'azim" (Glory be to my Lord the Mighty) and to struggle in order to grow its roots in our hearts, and in order to raise our head from ruku' with the hope of attaining Allah's mercy by repeating our mention of the greatness of Allah.

Sujud (prostration)

In this state, human beings represent the worship of the angels who serve Allah in sujud continuously and reptiles which seem to be in a constant state of prostration all their lives.

Prostration (sujud) is to abandon everything other than Allah (SWT) by saying, "Subhana rabbiyal a'la" (Glory be to my Lord the Most High) in modesty and awe before Allah's flawless beauty, brilliance, holy names and attributes. "A slave becomes nearest to his Rabb (Lord) when he is in prostration. So increase supplications in prostration." (Muslim)

Qa'da (sitting)

In this state, human beings represent the worship of the angels who serve Allah sitting, and also of the mountains, as rocks seem by their very shape to be sitting. A human being confirms that everything he owns belongs to Allah by reciting the tahiyyah (greeting) in this sitting position. He renews his faith by declaring the kalimah shahadah ("There is no God but Allah and Muhammad is His Messenger"). In salah there is a kind of Mi'raj for a believer, as the words of the tashahhud recall the holy conversation between Allah (swt) and the Prophet Muhammad during the Mi'raj (the Prophet's night journey and ascension).

SHORT 6 SURAHS IN QURAN

SURAH AL-ASR

بِسْمِ اللهِ الرَّحْمَٰنِ الرَّحِيمِ
وَالْعَصْرِ ۞ إِنَّ الْإِنْسَانَ لَفِي خُسْرٍ ۞ إِلَّا الَّذِينَ
ءَامَنُوا وَعَمِلُوا الصَّٰلِحَٰتِ وَتَوَاصَوْا بِالْحَقِّ وَ
تَوَاصَوْا بِالصَّبْرِ ۞

Bismillaahir-rahmaanir-raheem
Wal Aasr (1) Inna al-insana lafee khusr (2) Illaalla theena amanu wa aamiluutha lihati watawa sawbil haqqi watawa sawbis sabr (3)

"In the name of Allah, the Most Beneficent, the Most Merciful" "I swear by declining day. Indeed everybody is at a loss, except those, who have accepted, carried on godly deeds, (good causes), commanded each other the veracity and maqam of sabr [humility for Allah, taking themselves away from the sin]" Except those who believe (in Islamic Monotheism) and do righteous good deeds, and recommend one another to the truth, and recommend one another to patience".

Surat Al-Asr (The Passing Time) summarises in a few words the main themes of the Holy Quran. This Surah says that we will be losers if we do not make the most of our time by filling it with good deeds. It is these good deeds that will help us in the Hereafter. Those who do not believe in Allah and do not do good deeds, or spent their lives in lies and hypocrisy, will one day lose all that they worked for. Those who do not struggle to establish or fight for the truth will end up being losers.

SURAH AL-KAUTHAR

بِسْمِ اللَّهِ الرَّحْمَٰنِ الرَّحِيمِ ۝
إِنَّا أَعْطَيْنَاكَ الْكَوْثَرَ ۝ فَصَلِّ لِرَبِّكَ وَانْحَرْ ۝ إِنَّ شَانِئَكَ هُوَ الْأَبْتَرُ ۝

Bismillaahir-rahmaanir-raheem
Innaa a'ataynaakal kawthar (1) Fasalli lirabika wanhar (2)
Inna shaani'aka huwal abtar (3)

"In the name of Allah, the Most Beneficent, the Most Merciful"
Verily, We have granted you (O Muhammad (saw)) AlKawthar (a river in Paradise). Therefore turn in prayer to your Lord and sacrifice (to Him only). Indeed, your enemy is the one cut off (loser).

Al-Kawthar is the name of a fountain in Jannah (Paradise). Almighty Allah (swt) has given the Prophet (saw) this fountain. AlKawthar means "The Abundance". Surah al-Kawthar tells us that Almighty Allah gave Prophet (saw) good things in abundance and excellences to which there are no limit. This Surah tells us about our Prophet Muhammad (saw) high status.
Some leaders of the Quraish made fun of Prophet (saw) when his young son, AL- Qasim passed away saying that he no longer had any sons to carry on his name and that he would be forgotten after he passes away. Allah (swt) promises in this Surah that the memory of the Prophet (saw) would continue forever and that all those who are his enemies will be forgotten.

SURAH AL-NAAS

بِسْمِ اللهِ الرَّحْمٰنِ الرَّحِيْمِ ۝
قُلْ أَعُوذُ بِرَبِّ النَّاسِ ۝ مَلِكِ النَّاسِ ۝ إِلٰهِ النَّاسِ ۝
مِنْ شَرِّ الْوَسْوَاسِ ۙ الْخَنَّاسِ ۝ الَّذِي يُوَسْوِسُ فِي
صُدُورِ النَّاسِ ۝ مِنَ الْجِنَّةِ وَالنَّاسِ ۝

Bismillaahir-rahmaanir-raheem
Qul a'oothu birabbinnas (1) Malikinnas (2) Ilaahinnas (3)
Min sharril waswaasil khanaas (4) Allathee yuwaswisu
fee sudoorinnaas (5) Minal jinnati wannas (6)

"In the name of Allah, the Most Beneficent, the Most Merciful"
"Say: I seek refuge with (Allah) the Lord of mankind. The King of mankind. The God of mankind. From the evil of the whisperer who withdraws. Who whispers in the breasts of mankind. Amongst jinn and men"

An-Naas means "The People". Surat An-Naas teaches us to place our trust in Allah (swt). It teaches us to seek Allah's protection against things that might affect us. We should not place our trust in man. Allah (swt) is our King or Ruler. The Surah warns us against the secret whispers of evil inside our hearts. It also warns us about the evil that may come from other men or invisible spirits. As long as we put ourselves in Allah's protection and we trust in Allah (swt), evil will not be able to affect us.

SURAH AL-FALAQ

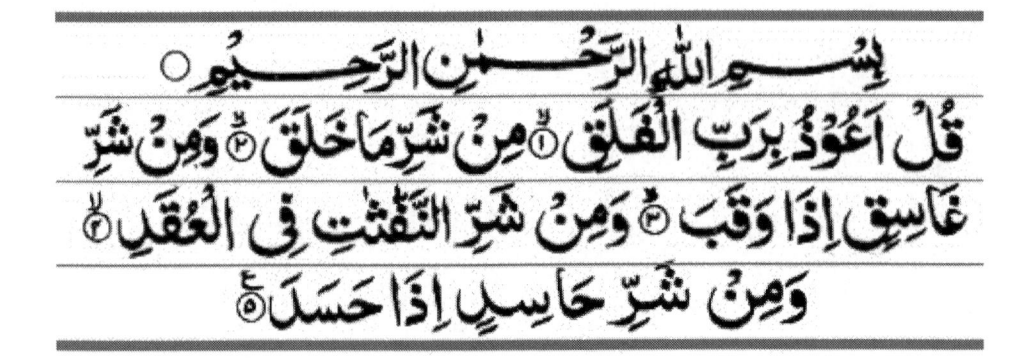

بِسْمِ اللَّهِ الرَّحْمَٰنِ الرَّحِيمِ
قُلْ أَعُوذُ بِرَبِّ الْفَلَقِ ۝ مِن شَرِّ مَا خَلَقَ ۝ وَمِن شَرِّ غَاسِقٍ إِذَا وَقَبَ ۝ وَمِن شَرِّ النَّفَّاثَاتِ فِي الْعُقَدِ ۝ وَمِن شَرِّ حَاسِدٍ إِذَا حَسَدَ ۝

Bismillaahir-rahmaanir-raheem
Qul a'oothu birabbil falaq (1) Min sharri maa khalaq (2) Wamin sharri ghasiqin ithaa waqab (3) Wamin sharrin-naffaathaati fil'uqad (4) Wamin sharri haasidin ithaa hasad (5)

"In the name of Allah, the Most Beneficent, the Most Merciful"
Say: "I seek refuge with (Allah) the Lord of the daybreak. From the evil of what He has created. And from the evil of darkness when it settles. And from the evil of the witchcrafts when they blow in the knots. And from the evil of the envier when he envies.

Surat Al-Falaq (The Dawn) teaches us to seek shelter in Allah (swt) from every kind of evil of nature. It teaches us to seek Allah's protection from all dark and evil plotting. This Surah also tells us that those who are sincere worshippers of Allah (swt) must be careful of the envious people who are the worst of peoples.

SURAH AL-IKHLAS

بِسْمِ اللَّهِ الرَّحْمَٰنِ الرَّحِيمِ
قُلْ هُوَ اللَّهُ أَحَدٌ ۝ اللَّهُ الصَّمَدُ ۝ لَمْ يَلِدْ وَلَمْ يُولَدْ ۝ وَلَمْ يَكُن لَّهُ كُفُوًا أَحَدٌ ۝

Bismillaahir-rahmaanir-raheem
Qul huwallaahu ahad (1) Allaahussamad (2) Lam yalid walam yoolad (3) Walam yakullahu kufuwan ahad (4)

"In the name of Allah, the Most Beneficent, the Most Merciful"
"Say He is Allah, (the) One. Allah the eternal and absolute. He begets not, nor was begotten. And there is none comparable or coequal unto Him.

Surah Al-Ikhlas is one of the most important Surah of the Holy Quran because it tells us about what we should believe about Allah (swt). Al-Ikhlas means "The Purity of Faith". When the Makkans, the Jews and the Christians asked the Holy Prophet (saw) about Allah Ta'ala, he used to answer them with this Surah. Our Prophet Muhammad (saw) used to recite this Surah often in his Salaah. He also said that by reciting this Surah a Muslim will be in love with Almighty Allah.

SURAH AL-KAFIRUN

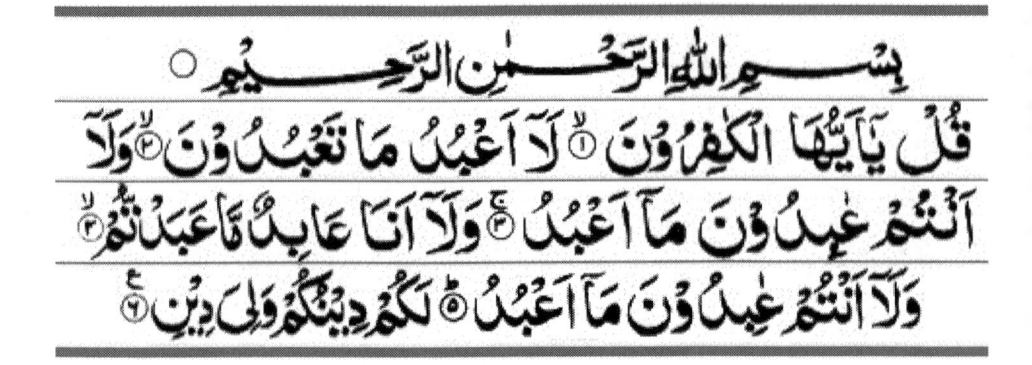

بِسْمِ اللَّهِ الرَّحْمَٰنِ الرَّحِيمِ
قُلْ يَٰٓأَيُّهَا ٱلْكَٰفِرُونَ ۝ لَآ أَعْبُدُ مَا تَعْبُدُونَ ۝ وَلَآ أَنتُمْ عَٰبِدُونَ مَآ أَعْبُدُ ۝ وَلَآ أَنَا۠ عَابِدٌ مَّا عَبَدتُّمْ ۝ وَلَآ أَنتُمْ عَٰبِدُونَ مَآ أَعْبُدُ ۝ لَكُمْ دِينُكُمْ وَلِىَ دِينِ ۝

Bismillaahir-rahmaanir-raheem
Qul ya ayyuhal kafirun (1) La a'budu ma Ta'budun (2) Wala antum abidunama a'bud (3) Wala ana abidumma abattum (4) Wala antum abidunama a'bud (5) Lakum dinukum waliyadin (6)

"In the name of Allah, the Most Beneficent, the Most Merciful"
"Say, O disbelievers. I do not worship what you worship. Nor are you worshippers of what I worship. Nor will I be a worshipper of what you worship. Nor will you be worshippers of what I worship. For you is your religion, and for me is my religion"

The Makkans wanted to make deals with Prophet (saw) to change the religion of Islam so that they will find it easier to follow. In one of the deals some people said that they will worship
Allah (swt) only for one year if the Prophet (saw) would worship their idols the next year, and they could continue to take
turns year after year. So Allah (swt) revealed Surah Al-Kaafiroon (The Unbelievers) to make it clear to the Quraish that it was not possible. Our Prophet Muhammad (saw) recited this Surah openly in public at every place to tell the Kufaar that the Muslims and the Kaafirs were not going to compromise as both their religions were not the same.

CONGREGATIONAL PRAYER AT HOME (STANDINGS)

Father and Son only

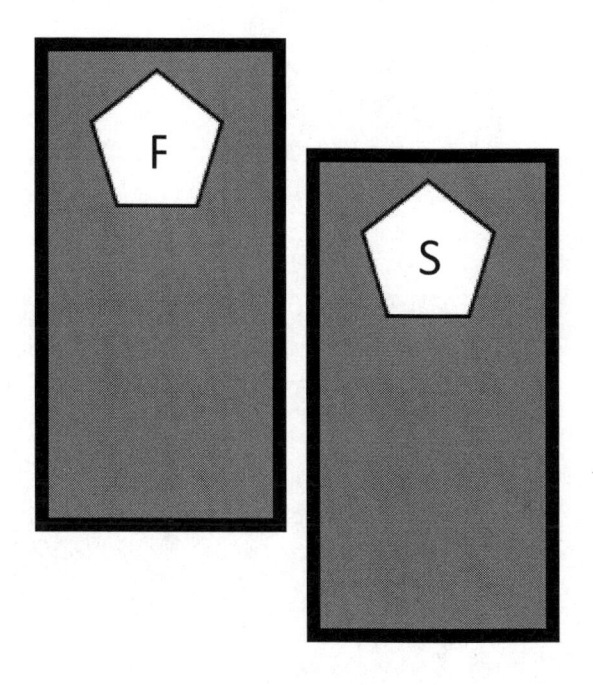

The father will lead the prayer, with the son slightly behind him on the right

Father and more than one male

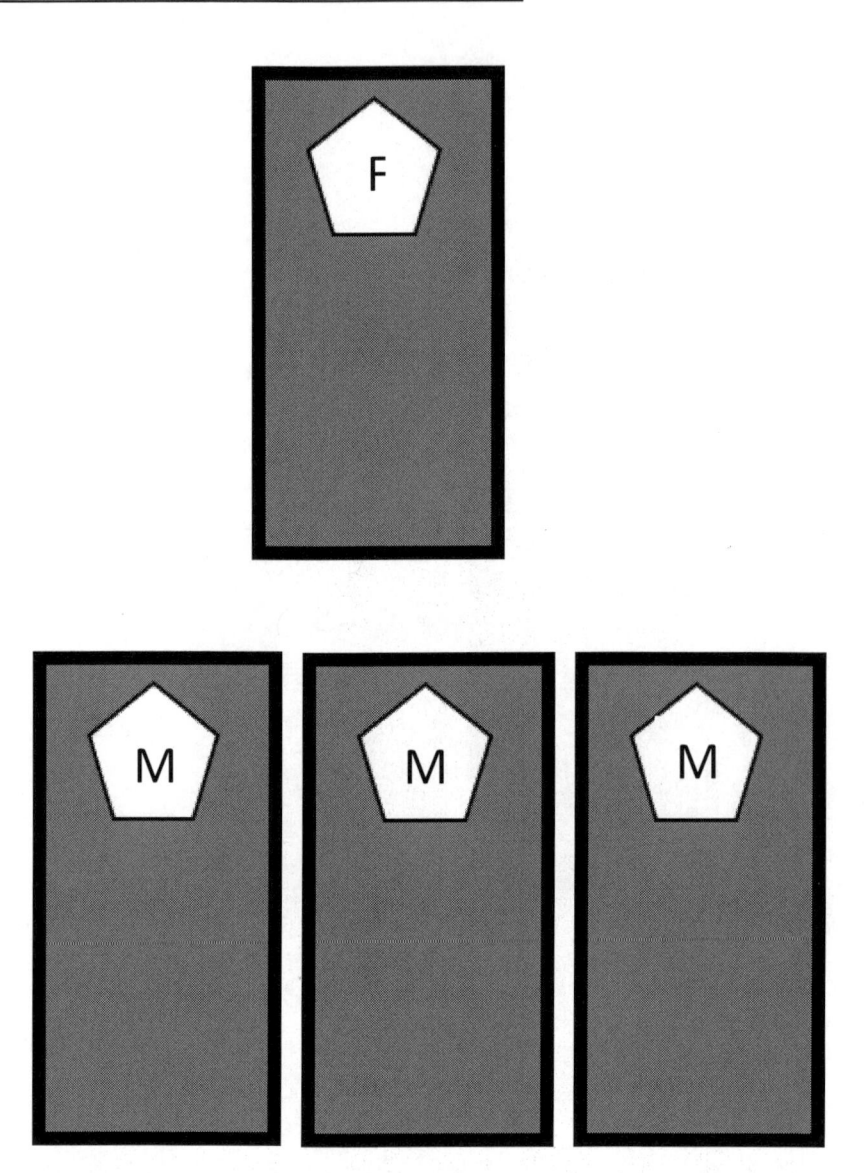

The father will lead the prayer, with the other males in a straight row behind him

Husband and Wife/Daughter only

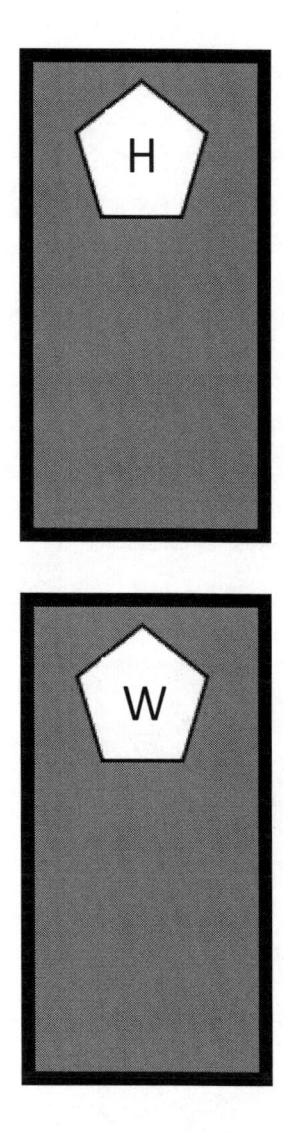

The husband will lead the prayer, and the wife a full row behind. The husband will give the iqamah and lead

Husband, Wife and one male child

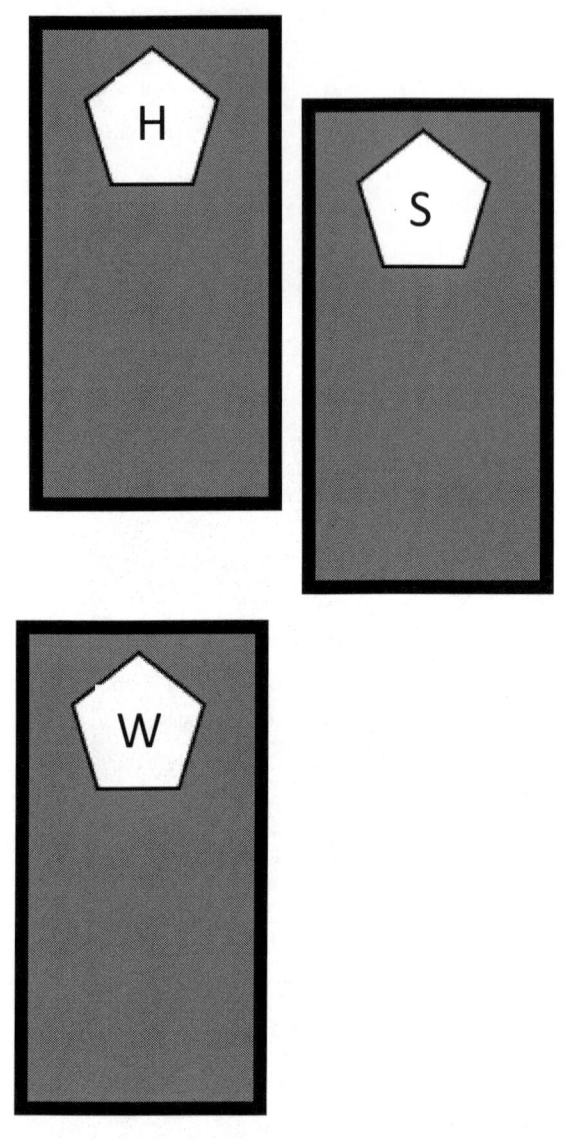

The husband will lead the prayer, and the child slightly behind on the right, The wife will be on separate row behind.

Husband, Wife and male child

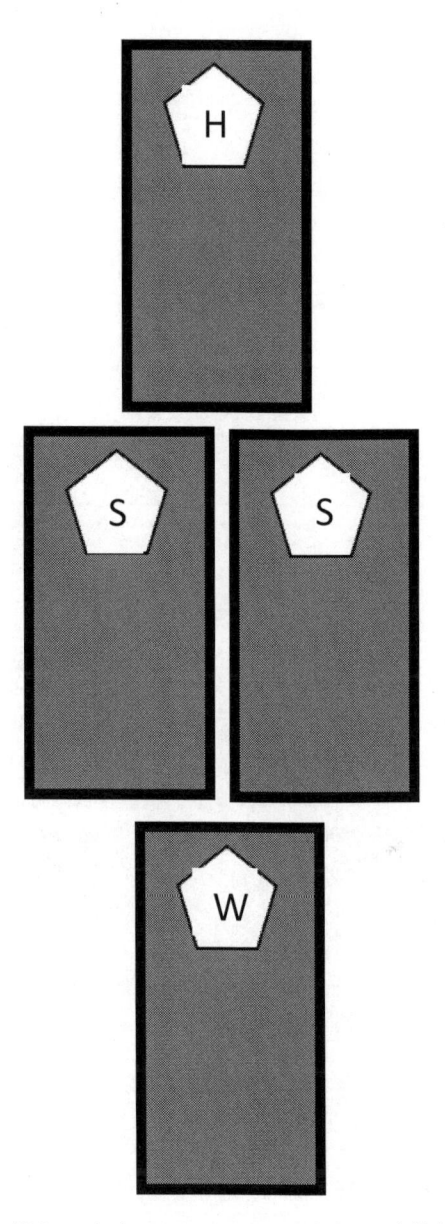

The husband will lead the prayer, and the children a row behind, The wife will be on separate row behind the children.

Husband, Wife and male child

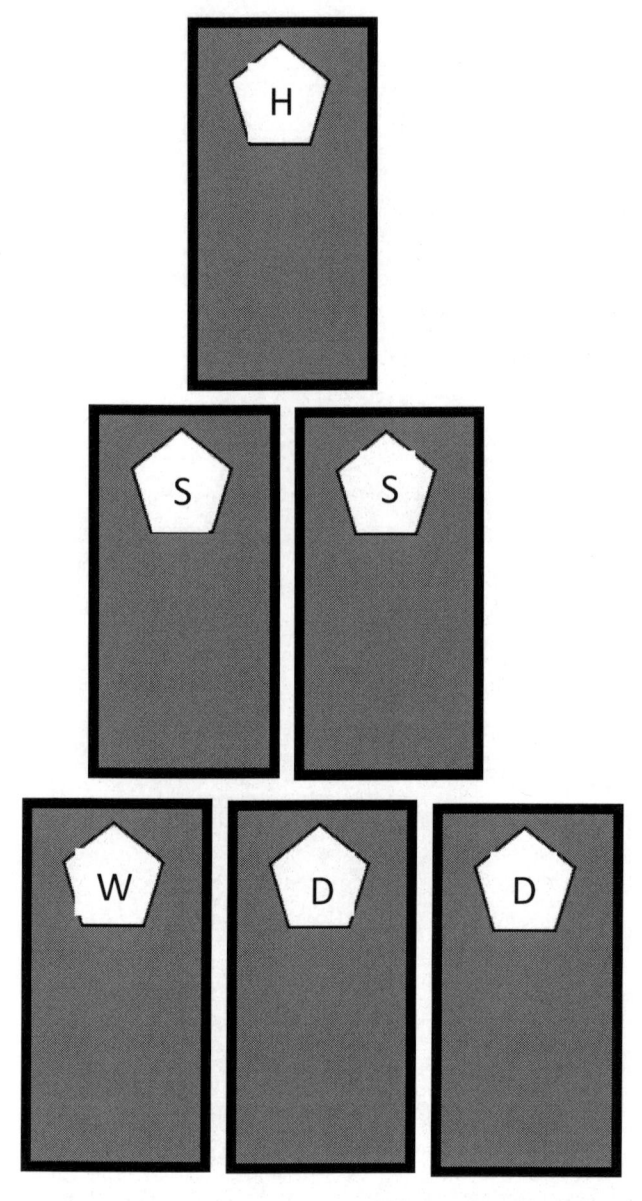

The husband will lead the prayer, and with male children a row behind,The wife and female children will be on separate row behind the male children.

MY SALAH TRACKER

Month: Week:

	SAT	SUN	MON	TUES	WED	THU	FRI
FAJR							
ZUHR							
AS'R							
MAGHRIB							
ISYA'							

Prophet Muhammad asked:
"which deed was best."

Prophet Muhammad (saw) said:
"The prayer at its appointed hour".

(Sahih Muslim)

MY SALAH TRACKER

Month: Week:

	SAT	SUN	MON	TUES	WED	THU	FRI
FAJR							
ZUHR							
AS'R							
MAGHRIB							
ISYA'							

Prophet Muhammad (saw) used to seek refuge in Allah(swt) from laziness that he used to mention it daily in this dua:

"O Allah, I take refuge in You from anxiety and sorrow, weakness and laziness, miserliness and cowardice, the burden of debts and from being over powered by men." [Sahih Bukhari]

MY SALAH TRACKER

Month: Week:

	SAT	SUN	MON	TUES	WED	THU	FRI
FAJR							
ZUHR							
AS'R							
MAGHRIB							
ISYA'							

Prophet Muhammad asked:
"which deed was best."

Prophet Muhammad (saw) said:
"The prayer at its appointed hour".

(Sahih Muslim)

MY SALAH TRACKER

Month: Week:

	SAT	SUN	MON	TUES	WED	THU	FRI
FAJR							
ZUHR							
AS'R							
MAGHRIB							
ISYA'							

"If you want to focus more on Allah in your prayers, focus more on Him outside your prayers."

(Yasmin Mogahed)

MY SALAH TRACKER

Month: Week:

	SAT	SUN	MON	TUES	WED	THU	FRI
FAJR							
ZUHR							
AS'R							
MAGHRIB							
ISYA'							

Prophet Muhammad (saw) asked:

"By Him in Whose Hand my life is, it is better for anyone of you to take a rope and cut the wood (from the forest) and carry it over his back and sell it (as a means of earning his living) rather than to ask a person for something and that person may give him or not."

[Sahih Bukhari]

MY SALAH TRACKER

Month: Week:

	SAT	SUN	MON	TUES	WED	THU	FRI
FAJR							
ZUHR							
AS'R							
MAGHRIB							
ISYA'							

One of the greatest pieces of advice given by Prophet Muhammad (saw) was:

"The most beloved actions to Allah are those performed consistently, even if they are few."

[Sahih Bukhari]

MY SALAH TRACKER

Month: Week:

	SAT	SUN	MON	TUES	WED	THU	FRI
FAJR							
ZUHR							
AS'R							
MAGHRIB							
ISYA'							

"And whoever fears Allah – He will make for him a way out and will provide for him from where he does not expect. And whoever relies upon Allah – then He is sufficient for him. Indeed, Allah will accomplish His purpose. Allah has already set for everything a [decreed] extent."

[Qur'an, 65: 2-3]

MY SALAH TRACKER

Month: Week:

	SAT	SUN	MON	TUES	WED	THU	FRI
FAJR							
ZUHR							
AS'R							
MAGHRIB							
ISYA'							

"Indeed, Allah will not change the condition of a people until they change what is in themselves."

[Qur'an, 13:11]

MY SALAH TRACKER

Month: Week:

	SAT	SUN	MON	TUES	WED	THU	FRI
FAJR							
ZUHR							
AS'R							
MAGHRIB							
ISYA'							

"After asking Allah to guide you to the straight path, don't just stand there ... start walking!"

(Albaz Poetry)

MY SALAH TRACKER

Month: Week:

	SAT	SUN	MON	TUES	WED	THU	FRI
FAJR							
ZUHR							
AS'R							
MAGHRIB							
ISYA'							

"Yesterday I was clever, so I wanted to change the world. Today I am wise, so I am changing myself."

(Rumi)

MY SALAH TRACKER

Month: Week:

	SAT	SUN	MON	TUES	WED	THU	FRI
FAJR							
ZUHR							
AS'R							
MAGHRIB							
ISYA'							

"The capacity to learn is a gift; the ability to learn is a skill; the willingness to learn is a choice."

(Islamic Thoughts)

MY SALAH TRACKER

Month: Week:

	SAT	SUN	MON	TUES	WED	THU	FRI
FAJR							
ZUHR							
AS'R							
MAGHRIB							
ISYA'							

"Allah knows exactly what to give you to help you return to Him. The events in your life are purposeful, appropriate & non-random."

(Shaykh Hamza Yusuf)

MY SALAH TRACKER

Month: Week:

	SAT	SUN	MON	TUES	WED	THU	FRI
FAJR							
ZUHR							
AS'R							
MAGHRIB							
ISYA'							

"My sin burdened me heavily. But when I measured it against Your Grace, O Lord, Your forgiveness came out greater."

(Imam Shafii)

MY SALAH TRACKER

Month: Week:

	SAT	SUN	MON	TUES	WED	THU	FRI
FAJR							
ZUHR							
AS'R							
MAGHRIB							
ISYA'							

"O Allah! Open for me my chest (grant me self-confidence, contentment, and boldness)."

[Qur'an, 20:25]

MY SALAH TRACKER

Month: Week:

	SAT	SUN	MON	TUES	WED	THU	FRI
FAJR							
ZUHR							
AS'R							
MAGHRIB							
ISYA'							

"And if there comes to you from Satan an evil suggestion, then seek refuge in Allah. Indeed, He is the Hearing, the Knowing."

[Qur'an, 41:36]

MY SALAH TRACKER

Month:　　　　　　　Week:

	SAT	SUN	MON	TUES	WED	THU	FRI
FAJR							
ZUHR							
AS'R							
MAGHRIB							
ISYA'							

"And whoever fears Allah – He will make for him a way out and will provide for him from where he does not expect. And whoever relies upon Allah – then He is sufficient for him. Indeed, Allah will accomplish His purpose. Allah has already set for everything a [decreed] extent."

[Qur'an, 65: 2-3]

MY SALAH TRACKER

Month: Week:

	SAT	SUN	MON	TUES	WED	THU	FRI
FAJR							
ZUHR							
AS'R							
MAGHRIB							
ISYA'							

"Strange are the matters of believers. For him there is good in all his affairs, and this is so only for the believer. When something pleasing happens to him, he is grateful (shukr), and that is good for him; and when something displeasing happens to him he is enduring patience (sabr) and that is good for him

(Sahih Muslim)

MY SALAH TRACKER

Month: Week:

	SAT	SUN	MON	TUES	WED	THU	FRI
FAJR							
ZUHR							
AS'R							
MAGHRIB							
ISYA'							

Prophet Muhammad (saw) said:

"No man fills a container worse than his stomach. A few morsels that keep his back upright are sufficient for him. If he has to, then he should keep one-third for food, one-third for drink and one-third for breathing."

[At-Tirmidhi]

MY SALAH TRACKER

Month: Week:

	SAT	SUN	MON	TUES	WED	THU	FRI
FAJR							
ZUHR							
AS'R							
MAGHRIB							
ISYA'							

Prophet Muhammad (saw) said:

"If a Muslim plants a tree or sows seeds, and then a bird, or a person or an animal eats from it, it is regarded as a charitable gift (sadaqah) for him."

(Sahih Bukhari)

MY SALAH TRACKER

Month: Week:

	SAT	SUN	MON	TUES	WED	THU	FRI
FAJR							
ZUHR							
AS'R							
MAGHRIB							
ISYA'							

"There are two blessings which many people lose: (They are) health and free time for doing good."

(Sahih Bukhari)

MY SALAH TRACKER

Month: Week:

	SAT	SUN	MON	TUES	WED	THU	FRI
FAJR							
ZUHR							
AS'R							
MAGHRIB							
ISYA'							

Prophet Muhammad (saw) said:

"Take benefit of five before five:
Your youth before your old age,
Your health before your sickness,
Your wealth before your poverty,
Your free-time before your preoccupation and
Your life before your death."

[Mustadrak Al-Haakim]

MY SALAH TRACKER

Month: Week:

	SAT	SUN	MON	TUES	WED	THU	FRI
FAJR							
ZUHR							
AS'R							
MAGHRIB							
ISYA'							

"If you are grateful, I shall certainly give you increase"

[Qur'an, 14:7]

MY SALAH TRACKER

Month: Week:

	SAT	SUN	MON	TUES	WED	THU	FRI
FAJR							
ZUHR							
AS'R							
MAGHRIB							
ISYA'							

"Actions are by their intentions"

[Sahih Bukhari and Muslim]

MY SALAH TRACKER

Month: Week:

	SAT	SUN	MON	TUES	WED	THU	FRI
FAJR							
ZUHR							
AS'R							
MAGHRIB							
ISYA'							

"Then when you have taken a decision, put your trust in Allah."

[Qur'an, 3:159]

MY SALAH TRACKER

Month: Week:

	SAT	SUN	MON	TUES	WED	THU	FRI
FAJR							
ZUHR							
AS'R							
MAGHRIB							
ISYA'							

"If Allah puts anyone in the position of authority over the Muslims' affairs and he secludes himself (from them), not fulfilling their needs, wants, and poverty, Allah will keep Himself away from him, not fulfilling his need, want, and poverty."

[Abu Dawud]

MY SALAH TRACKER

Month: Week:

	SAT	SUN	MON	TUES	WED	THU	FRI
FAJR							
ZUHR							
AS'R							
MAGHRIB							
ISYA'							

"The Salah with jama'a (congregation) is 27 times more rewarding than the solitary (individual) prayer."

[Sahih Bukhari]

Purpose of this book

Every praise and thanks is due to Allah, and may His Peace and Blessings be upon His last and final Messenger, Prophet Muhammad (saw).

This book 'A Step-by-Step Instructional Guide to Pray', is written in order to help children revert Muslims easily understand the 2nd pillar of Islam, and to make it easy for them to establish it in a proper manner on daily lives.

As-Salah is the parameter to distinguish between belief and disbelief, still we fail to convey this to many who accept Islam, who ultimately fail to establish As-Salah in their daily life as Muslims.

In this book we attempt to help our new brothers and sisters in Islam, understand this important pillar of Islam, and help them become part of the congregation of Muslims.

(swt) mentioned after Allah's name, is read as "Subhanahu Wa Ta'ala", Meaning 'The most Glorified, The Most High'

(saw) mentioned after the Prophet's name, is read as "Sallallahu Alayhi Wasallam", meaning 'May Peace and Blessings be upon him'

Made in the USA
Columbia, SC
13 February 2025